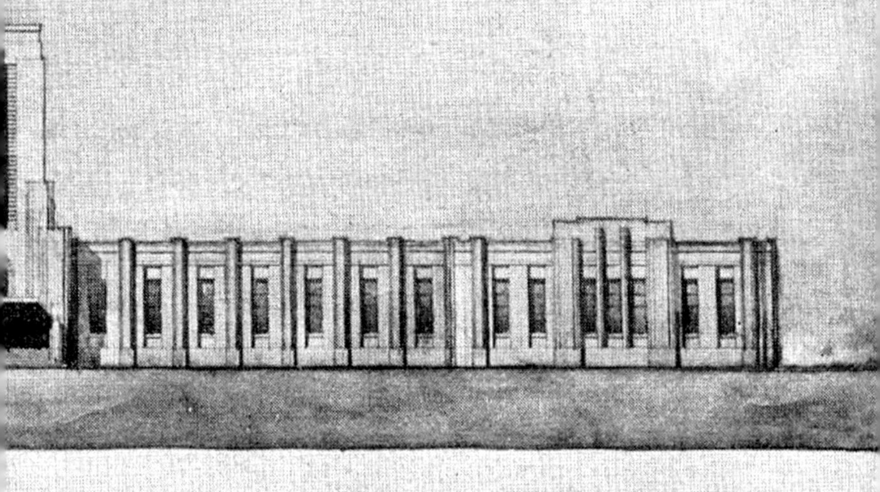

ARCH LABORATORIES.

EMICAL FUEL AND REFRACTORIES DEPARTMENTS AND THE TECHNICAL LIBRARY

LIMITED

A STEEL MAN IN INDIA

by

JOHN L. KEENAN

with the collaboration of

LENORE SORSBY

Introduction by

LOUIS BROMFIELD

First published by Victor Gollancz in 1945
Gollancz is an Hachette UK imprint
This edition © 2018 Hachette India, an Hachette UK company
www.hachetteindia.com

'Preface to the 2018 reissue' © Tata Steel
Jacket and endpaper images © Tata Steel

The dust-jacket design is a recreated reproduction of the original Gollancz edition published in 1945, as is the blurb on the jacket flaps and the text is exactly as in the original.

edition reissued for gifting and private circulation only and is not for sale.

SRD

All rights reserved. No part of the publication may be reproduced, stored in a retrieval system (including but not limited to computers, disks, external drives, electronic or digital devices, e-readers, websites), or transmitted in any form or by any means (including but not limited to cyclostyling, photocopying, docutech or other reprographic reproductions, mechanical, recording, electronic, digital versions) without the prior written permission of the publisher, nor be otherwise circulated in any form of binding or cover other than that in which it is published and without a similar condition being imposed on the subsequent purchaser.

Print edition ISBN 978-93-5009-570-6
Ebook ISBN 978-93-5009-588-1

Hachette Book Publishing India Pvt. Ltd
4th & 5th Floors, Corporate Centre,
Plot No. 94, Sector 44, Gurugram – 122 003, India

Printed in India by Manipal Technologies Limited

TO

THE MEN WHO—IN NO MEAN WAY—
HELPED TO BUILD AND OPERATE THE LARGEST
STEEL PLANT IN THE BRITISH EMPIRE

CONTENTS

Preface to the 2018 reissue

I am delighted that John L. Keenan's memoir, captured in *A Steel Man in India,* is seeing a revival. This is not just the story of a man, incredibly fascinating though he was. Keenan can claim to be the only American (Irish-American, to be precise) to have a cricketing stadium named after him. While that's some interesting trivia, the larger point is that the man was important enough to merit this happening.

This book, a business history classic, will tell you his story, but I think it goes beyond that. In these pages lies the story of the making of modern India. Keenan was joined by colleagues not just from India, but also from Germany and Britain, to create what became the face of modern India - Jamshedpur. This is a story that has as much relevance today as it did in the early 1940s, when the book was first published.

Whether you're a business history buff or a biography fan or just interested in the stories that have played a part in Indian history, this book will have something for you. Rich in anecdote and detail, this is a book that will continue to inform, entertain and, I dare say, enlighten us.

T.V. Narendran
CEO and Managing Director, Tata Steel

INTRODUCTION

I REMEMBER THAT I first met Jack Keenan exactly eleven years ago in March, for it was the day after the banks closed in America, and the news reached me in the depths of the jungles of Cooch Behar, one of the smaller Indian States, lying under the eaves of the Himalayas on the north edge of Bengal. It was late afternoon, and we had got two panthers and a big leopard, when across one of the dry rice-paddy fields, we saw an elephant, ridden by a *mahout* and carrying a passenger, coming towards us. Our own *mahouts* stopped a fresh drive and waited, for all of us were aware that a courier elephant could only bring news of importance. When the elephant came nearer I saw that the passenger clinging to the roped mattress was my friend Raschid Baig, who had come to Cooch Behar with us for the shooting. The elephant was an old female pet called Sita, some ninety-five years old, with her hide hanging in folds and wrinkles. The driver pushed her in between my elephant and that of the Maharanee, and Raschid said, "All banks have been closed in America. I just heard it over the radio. It means that I shall have to take the morning train to Calcutta."

There was something especially startling about the news coming by elephant courier in the midst of that beautiful jungle just under the vast, snow-covered expanse of Kittenjanga. It gave me a sudden sense of something which a few years later everyone in the world would feel—a sense of how much the world had shrunk and how important the United States was as a nation. Even here in the semi-feudal state ruled by a beautiful and wilful Maharanee Regent who still held audiences of her subjects, you could no longer escape either news or what touched people on the other side of the world.

In the morning of the next day I left with Raschid by the slow, antiquated, narrow-gauge railway that wandered down the wet, jungly valleys of Bengal to Calcutta. Raschid was a Moslem Indian educated at Oxford and, like many Moslem Indians, full of vitality and wit and friendliness and intelligence. On the long, slow trip we talked a great deal about the future of India, of America, and of a world changing so rapidly in the East that thought could scarcely keep pace any longer with the changes. In all our talk it never once occurred to us that some day, not too far away, the Japanese would be in Java, Sumatra, Singapore, Burma, on the very borders of this Bengal through which we were passing.

At the time I was still new in India. It was for me a new and wonderful place with a fabulous past and an immense, indeed a limitless future. Somehow, in our conversation, we came round presently to the subject of the Indian's abilities for finance, industry, and agriculture, when Raschid said suddenly, "Why don't you go up to Jamshedpur? I'll show you something there. Jack Keenan is a great friend of mine, and he and Mrs. Keenan would love to have you stay with them."

I asked, "What is Jamshedpur and who is Jack Keenan?"

I think Raschid was a little astonished and a little hurt over my ignorance. He said, "Jamshedpur is the tenth greatest steel centre in the world. Keenan is General Manager—a kind of Irish-

American Maharaja. The mills are all owned by Indian capital and largely run by American engineers until Indians themselves are trained to take over."

I reflected for a moment. To accept such an invitation, especially at second hand, meant the sending of telegrams, the shifting of plans, all of which in India meant delays, complications, and disappointments. But I thought, "This is the India I want to see most—the India of the future." I was already aware of an immense stirring, a coming-to-life over the whole of the East. I thought, "This is what I came out here to see." And so I said, "Yes. I think I'd like to."

And so in that hot little railway carriage on a narrow-gauge jungle railway in North Bengal began an adventure which opened up a whole new vein of richness in living and the understanding of many things which later on I should never otherwise have understood.

The key to it was, I think, Jack Keenan and his wife Mary.

Luckily we found him in Calcutta, and two days later we were aboard the Calcutta-Jamshedpur Express with Jack and several friends. Most of them were the lusty kind of American engineers you find scattered through the East. One of them, I remember, was a big fellow from the Tennessee Mountain country called Day. He said that when he put on shoes for the first time at the age of sixteen, "he felt like he was chained to the ground". The others on the party were Indians, business men, who had to do with the mills.

Lustiest of all the engineers was Keenan. A big Irishman, he liked people and whisky and horse-racing, and most important of all he liked Indians, all kinds of Indians—much the way I myself came to like them. He could talk a mile a minute and was a great story-teller. He told gusty Rabelaisian stories better than anyone I ever met. And I can say that never before or since have I encountered anywhere such vitality.

After the custom of the East, we drank our way to Jamshedpur, but in spite of the gin and whisky and the good stones, I managed to keep one eye on the rich, beautiful Bengal country. After a couple of hours we came out of Bengal into Bihar and Orissa, and the country changed. It grew wilder and wilder, the villages smaller and farther apart, the lonely farms little more than clearings in wild jungle. And the people changed too. They no longer had the soft, pleasant good looks of the Bengali, sometimes touched by the hint of Chinese or Burmese blood. With each mile the people grew smaller, harder, darker, more savage in appearance.

When I remarked on this, Raschid, a great authority on Indian races and history, said, "Yes, we're getting into really wild country. Most of the people here are aborigines who believe in witch-doctors. Up around Jamshedpur they're all like that."

And then presently the night came down quickly and all you could see in the velvety blackness was an occasional yellow camp-fire or the glow, like that of a firefly, of a coconut-oil lamp in some half-hidden hut. In a few hours' ride we had come back to the very beginnings of mankind.

Then the most extraordinary thing happened to the inky-black landscape. There appeared in the sky ahead of the train and a little to the left an immense glow, with billowing clouds of smoke tortured and churning over and over in shades of rose and scarlet and grey and black. It was the kind of night spectacle sometimes provided by volcanoes like Stromboli, but more often by great steel cities like Mannheim or Pittsburgh or Birmingham.

I asked, "What is that?" and Raschid answered, "That's Jamshedpur."

"Working night shifts in these times?"

"Yes. They're doing a tremendous business. Their pig-iron is of such fine quality they ship it even to Philadelphia."

I watched the distant rosy spectacle for a time, thinking about all I had heard before in the West about Indians having no abilities and no Western sense of enterprise. Looking at Jack Keenan and the other American engineers and Raschid and the two other Indians with us, I thought about all the old banality and nonsense of the jingle about "East is East and West is West". And then the train pulled into the station of a great city of 100,000 people which had grown up about the mills—a vast industrial city as big as Gary, Indiana, set down in the midst of dense jungle and aboriginal people.

Jack Keenan had played a big part in the creation and continuance of the Jamshedpur Mills. He knew all the story from the beginning. But that is his story. He tells it in this book together with many other things which I doubt have ever been told about India before, certainly not in his own particular lusty fashion.

Seven years ago Jack Keenan resigned from the job of being the American Maharaja of Jamshedpur and came home to retire to a farm in Vermont. But when the war came he knew there was a job for him to do back in the East, and although he was well over age and entitled to rest, he never ceased trying to find his place. He fought Government red tape and delays, growing constantly more and more restless. And then two weeks before this was written I had a telephone call from Los Angeles at three in the morning. On the other end of the wire was Jack Keenan. I don't know how old Jack is, but he is no longer young. Over the wire his voice sounded like that of a boy. He had been celebrating again. For a moment he talked with great seriousness about leaving his wife and daughter, to whom he was devoted. And then with excitement he said, "This is it! I've got a job at last. Tomorrow

I'm off to Chungking." He was going back to the East again, to the people he knew and respected and loved.

This book is Jack's story. I think when you have read it you'll understand about Jack and that peculiar quality of warmth and understanding which long ago crossed the barriers of race, colour, and religion, of which so much is made, and which are, in reality, so senseless and unreal.

Louis Bromfield
1943

CHAPTER I

YOUNG MAN, OLD INDIA

In the year 1903 a British capitalist declined to help finance the proposed Tata Iron and Steel Company; he was so amused by the request that he said he would eat every pound of steel rails produced in India. Thirty-four years later, when he came out to Jamshedpur for a last tiger shoot and I told him how many millions of tons of steel, made to the rigid British Standard specifications, the Tata mills had turned out, he smiled and said, "I can see now that my appetite in the old days must have been enormous."

I had no need to tell him further what he already knew, that Tata's was the largest and the most modern steel plant in the British Empire, and the twelfth largest in the world.

He could see for himself the spacious, well-planned city of Jamshedpur which surrounds the steel plant, a city with parks and paved streets, hospitals and schools, water-works and sewers, temples and mosques, a race track and an airdrome, a big football stadium and a dozen playing-fields.

When I went to India, in 1913, the first blast furnace Tata's started with—and very up to date it was for that time—had been in operation for only two years. It produced 200 tons of pig-iron a day. Twenty years later four Tata furnaces were each averaging

825 tons a day; one of them ran an average of 1,100 tons daily for many months. In all the United States, so far as I know, there are only two such furnaces. And furnaces were my immediate interest at Tata's, for I had been hired by T. W. Tutwiler, who had been general foreman of blast furnaces in Gary, and my boss, to replace him in the same job at Tata's on a three-year contract. I stayed, however, for twenty-five years, the last eight as general manager of the whole works. In India, a general manager is to a company what a president is in the United States.

A man can see a lot in twenty-five years. What I saw was the transformation of the old cultural India into the new industrial India, with Tata's as the backbone of the country's growing industrialization.

Of course, the change had begun years before I got there. Pick up a yearbook of, say, the time of Victoria's Diamond Jubilee, and you'll see that some 14,000 Indians were studying abroad, but they were training to be doctors, lawyers, and members of other professions. You could count on the fingers of one hand the lads who were getting industrial or engineering training. But for years now not only has the number of students getting degrees been on the increase, but the percentage of those working in scientific lines has risen considerably. And more than any other single factor, the Tatas were responsible for the trend of India's youth towards science and industry. They founded the Institute of Science in Mysore, gave scholarships to European and American universities, and employed the most promising graduates in their many enterprises.

I was twenty-four years old in 1913, with schooling at the Boston Latin School and at Yale almost entirely centred on Homeric Greek, the Latin classics, and economics, instead of, as one might have expected, on chemistry and engineering. I had

had six months' experience with the old Wharton Iron Company, near Dover, New Jersey, learning about blast furnaces. But the Wharton Company was dying when I got my job there, mainly because it had to depend on its local low-grade magnetite ore and on high-priced Mesabi range hæmatite; and hauling the hæmatite from Minnesota had proved too expensive. Since hæmatite is Fe_2O_3, it is easier to reduce metallic iron from its oxide than from magnetite, Fe_3O_4.

Anyway, I jumped a train and landed in Gary, Indiana, back in the days of Halley's Comet, and about a week before Jack Johnson proved that Jim Jeffries could not make a come-back. I had two dollars in my pocket when I got to Gary, but I stayed there three years, the first one as an engineer on blast-furnace construction, the next two on operation in the same department, as foreman on old blast furnaces Nine and Ten.

During the time that I was learning my trade in Gary, a number of steel men began to leave companies in America to inaugurate in India the production of steel along modern lines. They were the pioneers. But when I signed up with Tata and set out to follow them, it wasn't so much of them or of their work I was thinking as of the Great Moghuls, of Kipling and *Dolls in a Teacup,* of Laurence Hope. Anticipation made that first trip out so vivid as to pale all the others by comparison. I thought often of Hope's lines about India, its—

> *Deep dark forests and poisoned trees,*
> *Its pains and passions that scorch and freeze.*

I remembered William Hickey and other writers of the eighteenth century. In Hickey's day an old square-rigger made the trip from London or Southampton to Calcutta in eleven months—that is, if it was a fast boat. The ship made a straight line for the coast of Brazil to take advantage of the prevailing winds. Livestock, chickens, and other stores were taken aboard in Brazil, and the ship was headed due south until it crossed the line of latitude running through the Cape of Good Hope. The course would then be set east to follow the southern trade winds, through the Indian Ocean and the Bay of Bengal, eventually bringing up at Madras, then Fort George, or Calcutta, then Fort William.

Even in my time, in the early 1910's, women never came up on deck before seven in the morning, because, if they did, they were likely to find the male passengers parading about in their pyjamas. Most of the men slept on deck. They were wakened at five o'clock when the Lascars commenced to swab the decks, and by six they had foregathered, still in pyjamas, in the dining-room for tea. Men from the China Seas, tea-planters from Assam, engineers and jute-brokers from Calcutta, policemen and High Court judges came for tea and remained for a pleasant hour of swapping yarns. One got a wonderfully colourful picture of India from the talk during morning tea.

One tale I remember came from a policeman who weighed about 260 lbs., and had a high-pitched voice that carried all over the ship with a sound like a high-speed saw cutting cold steel. He told us how he had captured the leader of a dacoit, or robber, band. He had concealed himself in a tree, and when the dacoit came stealthily along the path below, our policeman simply dropped from his perch on a giant branch onto the dacoit and, sitting there, shouted for his fellow officers. If I remember well, the dacoit chief was charged, among other things, with some three hundred murders.

Nowadays it is possible to get to India from New York by air in seven days, or two and a half days from London. I must be, as I'm often told, pretty old-fashioned, because no matter how unbearable the Red Sea can be, and usually is, I much prefer the long trip to India by water.

On that first voyage, back in 1913, I met a man, a veteran tea-trader, who impressed on me the wisdom of learning Hindi or Urdu, or both. I wasn't much worried about learning either. I had operated two large furnaces at Gary, and only two of my furnace men could speak English, and that very imperfectly. I had had Croats, Hungarians, Serbians, Austrians, Bessarabians, and even one Turk among my motley crew. With the exception of a few words here and there, I had never mastered any of their languages. I had, however, made sure to learn in all of their tongues the equivalent of the twelve onomatopoetic, monosyllabic, unprintable, Anglo-Saxon words.

My tea-trader friend assured me that I would have little difficulty with the Hindu language because I knew Latin and Greek thoroughly. And when I did get around to studying it, I found the grammar similar enough, since all three tongues are derived from Sanskrit. In fact, I soaked up both Urdu and Hindi like a new blotter. But that was later.

Meantime our ship had arrived in Port Said and my friend took me along to Simon Artz's shop and bought me a copy of *Hindustani Simplified* by Syed. Every traveller to the East remembers Simon Artz's, the huge department store on the waterfront which never closed its doors as long as a liner lay at anchor in the entrance to the Suez Canal.

I was to know Simon Artz's place well in later years, to know the faces of many of the shopgirls, all of whom were not only pretty, but could speak French, Arabic, English, and Hindustani. Whenever I went back to the States on leave, I would, like everybody else, leave my soiled tropical clothes at Artz's, silk suits, white duck suits, underwear, and shirts. Six months later, on my way back, my bag would be waiting for me, packed neatly with freshly laundered apparel. Since Suez is a duty-free port, a bottle of Christmas Night costing twenty-five dollars in New York could be bought at Artz's for three; Johnny Walker Black Label was around a dollar and forty cents; pure Havana cigars set you back five cents apiece.

All the old-timers on board that ship were mightily amused at the idea that I was going out to India to make steel in an Indian concern. Indians could weave cotton cloth and make jute gunny-bags, they said, but *steel*! Why, even Tata's was sure to close down within the year. These men belonged to the generation which thought all Indians were dumb and would always be dumb. With the sound of their good-natured jeers in my ears, I landed in a village which is now called Jamshedpur, in the province of Bihar, and went to work as a shift foreman on the blast furnaces with two other Americans and about 500 Indians. None of those Indian workmen was dumb. They all did their jobs conscientiously and efficiently, and we never had a misunderstanding.

But I soon realized that there was a gulf between me and my men and that there would be until I learned their language. In the whole lot of Indians only two spoke English. Whenever I needed to give an order I called one of them to me, told him what I wanted, he translated into Hindustani, and my instructions were carried out to the letter. But the men seemed to remain aloof, and aloofness and distrust are closely associated. I picked out two good teachers. One was a young Brahmin stove-tender of fair education who spoke English well and whose mother tongue was Hindi. Bagwanda Bagwar (nicknamed Brophy) was seventeen then and had been a widower since childhood; he could read and understand Sanskrit and his grasp of the abstract was of a high order.

One day, speaking of the mystery of life, he pointed to an electric-light bulb. Turning the switch on and off, he said, "The light we have just seen is life. Turn on the switch, we are born. Turn it off, we die. The electricity is there whether we see it or not. Life is there unseen also. Men and animals are proofs of life. They prove the existence of a maker, they prove God."

My other teacher was an Afghan, Abdulla Rahman Khan, who could speak pure Urdu, the language of the up-country Moslems. Although his knowledge of English was limited, he read the Koran and was a "prescriber of medicine". His race called him a holy man. Just before I met Abdulla, he had been confronted with a situation in his private life which paralleled the poem *Afridi Love* by Laurence Hope. But he dealt with it in his own way.

Returning home unexpectedly one day, he found his wife with a lover. Drawing out a long dagger, he struck hard and pinned the two hearts together with one blow, his fury adding strength to his sinewy arm. But he still desired to live, so he fled from his native Afghan hills and settled in Hindustan. There, had his wife's relatives followed him, he could have handled them according to the old law of an eye for an eye.

I knew another Khan, a man who belonged to the same clan as my Afghan teacher and came from the same district. He also was a leader of men, although he was small of stature and affected shirts and knee-breeches of black silk. From him I heard the story of my Afghan teacher's ancestry.

When Abdulla's grandmother was fifteen a neighbouring clan raided her tribe's territory in Afghanistan. She was carried away with the rest of the booty and given to the son of the raiding chief. This young man was not hard to look upon, but she could not forget that he was an enemy of her people. A few months after her capture, her tribe made a counter-raid and the girl and her warrior husband were brought home.

Ready to put her captor to death, the elders asked the girl if she had anything to say before the tribunal passed sentence. She had. Drawing the eyes of the tribunal to her condition with a gesture, she said, "If it be a son, let him who is the father live. But if it be a daughter, let him die slowly, without haste." It was a son and the captive was freed. The son grew to manhood and had a son who came to India. That son was my teacher.

The man who told me this story is dead now. I saw him die. It was near the close of the first World War and we were lining a blast furnace, dynamiting the residual conglomerate of carbon, slag, and iron, known as the salamander, from the hearth. We shot some four or five holes at the same time, and after the shots the Khan and I examined the results. Khan went to a hole that had misfired, and as soon as he touched the wire, the delayed explosion occurred. A sliver of iron ripped a clean cut across Khan's belly, and his intestines flowed out upon the ground. I stuffed them back and tied my shirt around him until we could get the man to the hospital. At his bedside, I asked what I could do for him. He said in a whisper, "Give me a cigarette, sahib, and light it for me. Don't leave me. I won't keep you long. I am dying, sahib. I know it. But it is great."

Slowly he took a few puffs, looked at me and smiled, then passed on to meet his prophets, Moses, Christ, and Mohammed. We buried him in a wooden box. Six months later, his tribe received permission to transfer his remains back to far-off Afghanistan. When the coffin was opened, there lay the Khan in peaceful sleep. The soil of Hindustan had not permitted the flesh to fall away. We sent him home.

Shortly after that we had to exhume the body of an American, also buried only a few months, to confirm his identity. We found nothing but bones and one gold tooth.

I had the greatest respect for my Afghan teacher. He pounded Urdu into my brain and saw to it that as we went along I learned something of the religion of his warlike ancestors, Mohammedanism. I noticed that whereas a westerner will designate his religion by saying he attends this or that church, there is actually no Mohammedan "church"; there is a Mohammedan faith. A man can live to a ripe old age and die a strict Mohammedan without ever having entered a mosque, by simply believing in and living according to the teachings of his master, and without any of the beautiful music, carpeted aisles, or Gothic edifices we westerners seem to need.

While studying Urdu, which uses the Persian alphabet, and Hindi, which is understood by nearly 150,000,000 people, I picked up quite a bit of Hindustani, the popular tongue which is a combination of them both with an admixture of many corrupted English words.

For example, since Hindus never eat beef, there is no word in Hindi for beefsteak. In Hindustani, however, there is *beefi istake.* Also *ishpunjrolli,* for sponge (or jam) roll. *Beefistew* is easy to figure out, but if your cook handed you a menu for approval and you found on it "— crab" and inquired what it meant, you would be told "very-bad-word-crab", hence, devilled crab. Then again, the Hindus never used matches before the arrival of the English. But when a British Tommy wanted to light his pipe and found himself without matches, he would say, "Give us a light". The Indian sepoy soon used the word *derseliy,* pronounced *dare sah lie,* or match—from the Sanskrit *diva,* light, and *sali,* stick.

During the first World War, the Indians loved the marching song *Tipperary* so much that they put their own Hindustani words to it. I heard a nautch girl singing them once while sitting with the Maharaja of Patiala at the wedding of his son. Phonetically spelled, the lyrics looked like this, they rhymed, and the meaning was approximately the same :

Burra dur high AH *Tipperary,*
Boat lumber cooch woe,
Burra dur high AH *Tipperary,*
Saaki PASS *Boat Chiney Ko.*
Ram ram AH *Piccadilly,*
Salaam, Leicester Square,
Burra Burra dur high AH *Tipperary,*
Lake-in deel hua PONCH *gee yah !*

Around a blast furnace work is intermittent. One finds plenty of time between casts to rest and to talk. After the men had cleaned up and prepared the sand-beds for the next tapping, they would sit about on those quiet, hot nights and listen to one of their number spin a yarn. My Afghan teacher was always called upon for a story, particularly one of those romances woven about the Great Moghuls. Listening to him, I walked with Shah Jehan and Mumtaz Mahal. I met Birbal, the seer, who held the precariously combined positions of Prime Minister and Court Jester at about the time that long-coated Puritans with funny hats were setting out on the voyage which was eventually to land them in Plymouth.

He described how Birbal and Akbar would sit of an evening on the terrace of the palace at Fatipur Sikri and amuse themselves with a game of chess. There, stretched out beneath their feet, was a chessboard somewhat larger than a modern tennis-court. On this "board" dancing-girls, in gala array, stood stiffly, representing the chess pieces, and were moved about by orderlies at a nod from Akbar or Birbal. Occasionally during the game, Abdulla said, Birbal might spot a man standing quietly in the background, a man in long, black, flowing garb, a Jesuit from the mysterious, unknown West. He would call the newcomer to him, for Akbar's favourite wife, Miriam, was a worshipper of Allah through the voice of Jesus of Nazareth and, with a wave of the hand, dismiss the human chess-pieces. Perhaps the moon rode high as the dancing-girls, the fragrance of their hair oil blending with the odour of frangipanni blossoms, sought out a cool, leafy bower and the arms of their lovers.

Then Akbar and Birbal would sit long hours and discuss theology with the foreigner, the Jesuit. And sometimes Miriam would join them. For Miriam was learned as well as beautiful. Like Moses, Mohammed, and Christ, Akbar wanted passionately to bind his people together in religion, to unite India.

Sometimes, gathered about the furnace, the night would be too hot for stories, especially to Nally Wallah and Ali Baba, who had not only heard often enough about the Great Moghuls, but who liked the centre of the stage themselves. Poor old Baba was a hashish smoker. Whenever the crowd congregated for a rest, Baba would put a pill into the brass nozzle which passed for a pipe, pick up a red-hot piece of slag with his hand leather, and press it into the bowl. He would work himself up by drawing a half-dozen deep breaths, meanwhile threshing his arms about like a Japanese wrestler preparing for a bout. Then, cupping his palm about the brass bowl to act as a pipe-stem, he would take two or three deep drags on the pipe, contemplate his audience for a moment, and suddenly jump up to start turning handsprings, landing now on one hand, now on the other. He would follow this with shadow boxing, until the other workmen demonstrated their appreciation with shouts and applause. Then he would sit down, pleased with his contribution.

Nally Wallah was like the pony who used to come into the circus ring with the trained horses and cut his own individual capers to steal the show. When Ali Baba had finished, Nally Wallah would challenge our champion wrestler, Guramdin (*guram*, hot—*din*, day; hence, Hot Day). Guramdin was a giant and his challenger a flyweight, but their insults were about equal. The way each man described his opponent and his ancestors would make your eyeballs crawl. Guramdin would threaten to tear Nally Wallah limb from limb and roast the pieces on the hot pig-iron, and to do other things that would make the tales of Glaucus and Diomede seem like bedtime stories for three-year-olds. Onlookers who had not watched this play before would slink away rather than see a particularly brutal murder done.

When the proper crescendo had been reached both men would remove whatever clothing they had on and stand forth in their loin-cloths. After a few moments of sparring about, they would charge into one another, and who would go down, with mighty groans, but Guramdin the giant. Seizing Nally Wallah, he would shout to the referees to search the flyweight. After a tussle the referee always found a pig-iron sample, weighing about a pound, claimed to have been concealed in Nally Wallah's fist or loin-cloth. Finally, after a jabbering contest which the workmen loved, both men would bury the hatchet and offer a bet that they could break ten beds of pig-iron faster than any four other men. They always won. I have seen those two break up fifty tons of iron, cast in the sand, and be none the worse for it.

Nobody expects blast-furnace men to be sissies; too many of them have died with their boots on. Up till a few years ago, open-hearth steel workers or steel rollers in England wouldn't patronize a pub where blast-furnace men went. The latter were only too prone to start a fight after a few drinks, while open-hearth fellows at that stage seem to have a strong desire for song. Our blast-furnace men were tougher than the proverbially tough structural-steel workers in the United States. I've seen many a fight between lumberjacks in the logging camps up on Moosehead Lake in Maine. They fought like lions, punching with their fists and butting with their heads, but they never used their boots, and if a man tried it, one of the surrounding crowd would take a hand and beat him to a pulp. But those woodsmen were lilies compared to the Americans who went to India to teach the Indian the art of bedding and breaking pig-iron, who used their feet as much as their fists and weren't above trying to gouge out an adversary's eyes. One night, in front of a gambling joint near Jamshedpur, I saw a man knock another down and then jump on his face with both feet.

Those boys had been trained in a hard enough school. In the old days in the United States a blast-furnace man worked a ten-hour shift for a week, then did a twenty-four-hour shift on Sunday, and followed that up with a week of fourteen-hour night shifts. There have been times when I took a newspaper and a dinner-pail with me on the long night shift and didn't have a chance to open either. I have often seen enormous, husky furnace operators collapse, white-eyed, in heat prostration. The only cure for a white-eyed man is sixteen hours' sleep under warm covers.

In those days blast furnaces still held most of their secrets. They hold some of them today. Two furnaces built side by side, identical in construction, can be as different in operation as day from night. One will break records and be called a "sweet thing". The other may never behave. That kind of furnace is always termed an "old bitch". And when those old furnaces went on the rampage, they were man-killers. Such a furnace is said to be "sick", and as late as 1910 there were still some furnace "doctors" operating in New Jersey and Pennsylvania, men who were called in to take complete charge until the sick furnace was in condition again. One doctor, I remember, also ran a blacksmith shop, where he made shoes for draft horses and mine mules. He did odd jobs of dynamiting, too, when required. It doesn't seem possible, now that only thirty-odd years ago, when the Tata furnaces were nearing completion, we in America were relying on people like that part-time horseshoer and dynamiter to doctor our sick furnaces.

It's human enough to resist change, and lots of experienced men in the business mistrusted the trend towards science in steel-making which began after the invention of the open-hearth steel process in 1878. One of the first steps was the installation of small chemical laboratories in plants to analyse pig-iron, which before that had been graded solely by the eye of the operator. The man whom all steel men of the day knew simply as "Captain" Jones complained bitterly to his boss, Andrew Carnegie, that those new-fangled chemists would ruin the business.

But with the advent of chemical laboratories and more exact, scientific producing methods, a different class of men came out of the colleges to explore the new opportunities in the steel game. Any strong young man who was scientifically inclined had high rewards waiting for him if he could stand the gaff. And to know that he had two great belching bitches under his care, to know that if he treated them right they would do their stuff, was a tremendous and exciting incentive. I believe Carl Langrebe, now vice-president of the Tennessee Coal and Iron Company, was the first American college graduate to break into the blast-furnace field. Before his time most of the furnace superintendents, even along the Atlantic seaboard, were not Americans, but Englishmen who had had some university training. It still takes guts to master your furnaces, but now science has brought under rigid control at least half a dozen of the variables that govern the behaviour of blast furnaces.

Many stories about those early American Tata workers in steel have been handed down in Jamshedpur, most of them exaggerated with time. But exaggerated or not, we like to forget some aspects of those first few years, in fact, to disown many of the men who came out to India, remained a few months or years, and then left. The superintendent who hired the original contingent of twenty-eight Americans for Tata's later excused himself for the type of men he brought out by saying that had he known the Indians would show the aptitude they did around the cast-houses, he could have hired half the number of Americans and could have chosen them more carefully. As it was, eighteen months after they arrived, all but eight of the Americans had left and Indians were doing all the strong-back work, making pig beds, breaking hot iron, handling it, and "keeping" the furnaces.

There were, however, some fine men too who were closely associated with the early days of steel in Jamshedpur, both American and Indian. Indra Singh was a Sikh who applied for construction work one day in 1910. He had had some experience in railway workshops up-country and was a fair machinist, but he wanted to be a contractor on construction. There were no vacancies. Singh stayed around town for a few days and learned that while the company was trying to amass a stock pile of some 50,000 tons at the plant, and not just piled along the rail sidings at the mines, the mining contractors in charge were falling down on the job. From the general manager, Bob Wells, the young Sikh got a job at the ore mines at one rupee, or thirty-seven cents, a day, with the opportunity of mining ore when he knew his way around. He left the next day and walked the forty-five miles to Gorumhasini to take over his post.

There are no underground shafts at any Tata mines. Once the surface soil is removed, the ore veins lie exposed and ready for the dynamiter. Then the ore is separated from the laterite or shale, loaded into tubs, and the miner is paid a flat rate for it per tub. If supervision is slack, the foreign material, which otherwise the miner would have to employ labourers to remove, is loaded right in with the ore. Before long Indra Singh was given a mining face to work as a contractor. He picked his labour carefully, male and female, gave them contracts at 20 per cent more than the prevailing rate, and produced more ore from his mining face than came from any of the others. Also we found by constant chemical analysis that the gangue, or foreign material, averaged less per tub in Singh's ore than in his competitors'. In this way Indra Singh, who had been willing to take a menial job at a few cents a day, laid the foundation for what was to become a fortune.

As a matter of fact, it shouldn't be surprising that Indians are good steel-makers. With access to the large deposits of ore ready to hand, Indians have manufactured iron for centuries, supposedly learning the art of smelting and forging from the ancient Chinese. Some scientists claim that weapons of the early Mediterranean peoples came from India. Homer tells of iron spears being brought to Troy by the princes of the East, and, incidentally, he was the first European writer to use the Sanskrit word *aes*, iron. While those iron spear-tips undoubtedly came from Persia, it is not unlikely that the metal was forged in India, just as some 2,000 years later the highly valued Damascene swords were tempered and shaped in Asia Minor from Indian iron.

Some thirty years ago, a metallurgist of standing spoke before a meeting of scientists in London on the Iron Pillar of Delhi, which was manufactured about A.D. 410. He said, "If this forging had been made even fifty years previous to the present time upon either side of the Atlantic, the front pages of the news sheets would have carried large headlines announcing the fact to an unbelieving world".

Now, scientists tell the exact truth as they see it (as compared with politicians, who are truthful to a certain degree). What this particular scientist actually said was that the iron-workers of India could boast of an achievement in forging which was still remarkable some 1,500 years later, and this at a time when the Roman legions, falling back upon Rome, left behind them a race which shortly before had had but one manufactured weapon, a stone hatchet. This implement served to ward off the Scots and other northern enemies; it was employed when the warriors on the Rhine would or would not give battle, according to whether the whirls and eddies of the Rhine were running clockwise or counter-clockwise. The hatchet was also useful in running down a man's breakfast—if the man were fleet enough of foot.

But the fact is that the Iron Pillar of Delhi has never to this day shown any signs of rust. There are several theories about the reason for this. Sir Robert Hadfield thinks it is because the makers included slag in the casting. Some say that the Indian women who embrace the column and try to touch hands around it, believing that if they succeed they will get the husband they want, have during the centuries rubbed enough of their body oil on the Pillar to preserve it. Personally, I am inclined to think that the old Indian iron-workers added some ingredient still unknown to our most advanced metallurgists.

I saw a mine once, in the wild up-country of Joda in Orissa, where men produced iron by the same primitive means their ancestors had used to work that same ore vein for untold generations. The tiny village was divided by the one, the main, street. On either side mud huts, sometimes whitewashed, oftener earth-coloured, clustered thickly. Each small house had one door, also small, and if the owner were prosperous, a window. The surrounding country was so wild that few white men had ever been seen there, and none at all until after the turn of the century, perhaps ten years before my visit. I knew about it because our prospectors, pushing inland from the Noamundi mines, which were then yielding half a million tons of iron ore a year, had found a rich lode in Joda, 1,700 feet above sea level.

When they discovered the place it was ridden with malaria and black-water fever. The death rate was often as high as sixty people per thousand from those causes alone. Now black-water fever has been stamped out entirely and malaria mortality is less than ten to every thousand natives.

We were not far from Noamundi as a bird would have flown, but separated by jungles and rocky hills, and centuries removed in ways of life and methods of work. Both were so crude in Joda, so ancient, that, watching them, I could almost think this very tribe of iron-workers, or *Loharis* in Sanskrit, had been the first to stumble on the art of wresting iron from the earth.

The miners were clothed economically in a yard or so of cotton cloth twisted around their loins. The women used the same material to conceal their bodies between the navel and the lower thigh. Boys and girls under twelve had only a woollen string about their bellies. These were primeval people, and therefore without sin. Why should they wear more? The women, incidentally, were the most beautifully built creatures I'd ever seen.

Under the workmen's hands a dozen small blast furnaces, of crude fire-clay and mud, turned out almost pure iron. A pair of bellows, like toy drums, supplied the air draught, which ran through bamboo poles to the hearth of the furnace. By standing upon the bellows, a young boy or girl could cover the intake hole of the drum with the heel, and by forcing the head of the bellows down, drive the air forward.

The process started with a few bushels of charcoal being charged into the furnace and lighted. The bellows would quickly raise the fire to a bright red heat. An old man, bent with age, would then throw handfuls of pulverized iron ore onto the incandescent charcoal. After an hour or so, the men would tear away the whole front of the furnace and draw out a spongy mass of iron and slag perhaps 50 lbs. or 75 lbs. in weight.

Now another group of men would hammer at this jagged lump, knocking off pieces of slag and other impurities. Later they cut the bar into lengths, reheated the pieces in a charcoal fire built in a small hole in the ground, hammered, and again reheated them. When, finally, the bar looked to be free from slag inclusions, it would be shaped into a hammer, a tip for a ploughshare, a knife, spear-point, or dagger.

I asked a furnace man how long the furnace had been in operation. He turned to his grandfather for information. The old man looked puzzled for a moment, shrugged his shoulders, and said simply, "Forever".

This slow, laborious, and ritualistic process had been handed down to them by the forbears of the men of Joda. Spear-tips for the Trojans, iron for Solomon's temple, and—who knows?—perhaps part of the Delhi Pillar came from this hilly village mine and were transported by water buffalo down the narrow valley paths to the sprawling plains of the cities below.

CHAPTER II

A PARSI HAS A DREAM

THE NAME TATA was originally a nickname, probably meaning hot-headed. Nusserwanji Tata, born in 1822 at Navsari, Bombay Presidency, a son of a Parsi of the priestly caste, and the fifteenth in descent to be called Tata, belied his name by his cool business judgment. It was Nusserwanji who founded the great Tata fortune, and founded it in cotton, not in iron or steel.

European biographers usually ascribe a great man's success partly to his inherited qualities. They will tell you that his frugality stems from an ancestor from the Highlands of Scotland, his deep religious conviction from a saintly grandmother from County Mayo. But we Americans ourselves frequently know little and care less about our forbears. An American racehorse owner will be familiar with the pedigree of his animals for thirty generations back, know that the brawn and bone descend from the sire and the virtues and vices through the dam, even though he may have no knowledge of his own great-grandparents. But the family tree of each male member of the priestly caste among the Parsis has long been noted down with care. So that we know pretty well where the Tata family were and what they were doing from almost the beginnings of recorded Eastern history. We know, too something of where Nusserwanji Tata got his integrity, his generous vitality, his fanatic devotion to an ideal.

The Parsis are an ancient people who lived originally in a part of Persia, known as Phars, and who followed the prophet Zoroaster. Their capital city of Persepolis, unsurpassed in the splendour of those times, was built by Tata ancestors and their fellow Parsis. Some historians tell us that Zoroaster lived during the reign of Hystapes. But, as historians will, they all differ, variously placing his time as 1300 B.C., 200 years before the fall of Troy, and around 500 B.C., or the fairly modern period of Cyrus. An erudite Parsi friend of mine, who likes his joke, even claims that Zoroaster forged the shoes for the winged Pegasus!

I like the earlier date for Zoroaster, since I'm told that the difference between Homeric and Attic Greek is negligible compared to the contrast between the chants of Zoroaster and the Persian script of Cyrus' time. And the same Parsi priests who are thoroughly conversant with the language in vogue during the reigns of Darius and Cyrus, confess that there are many Parsi chants and prayers still used at the String Ceremony, equivalent to our christening, at marriages and burial rites, which it is nearly impossible to translate with any certainty.

Parsis have often been called fire-worshippers, but fire is actually only an object of their veneration in so far as it represents purity. Some fire temples in India contain flame brought from far-off Persia in the course of various migrations. Sometimes the flame is obtained, one might say, straight from heaven.

Parsi priests who wish to start a new fire watch the forests during a storm. When lightning strikes a tree, they remove a burning fragment and, filling a flat metal tray with sandalwood, they hold the tray over the fire, but not in it. Thus a new fire is kindled. This ceremony is repeated nine times. The fire resulting from the ninth flame is deemed to be pure.

At any rate, the Parsis, and among them the Tata forbears, fought under Cyrus, side by side with the 10,000 Greeks; they battled the formidable war lord of ancient times, the man who would conquer the world but could not conquer his craving for alcohol, Alexander the Great. They were beaten, but not broken in spirit. In the year A.D. 530, when the Parsis waged war against Justinian, Tata ancestors led the cohorts who beat down the walls of Antioch and destroyed the city.

After the Arab invasion of Persia, many of the natives embraced Islam. Only the stalwart followers of Zoroaster, who preferred exile to the Crescent, remained true Persians. The blood of the Bombay Parsis today is as pure as that which flowed in the veins of the dwellers in Phars, or Pars, whence they derive their name. They are the children of an early migration settled at the port of Diu, a small island in the Gulf of Cambay. Their first fire temple was completed on the mainland of India in 721, at Sanjan, where the main part of that body of exiles lived for some 300 years. From that district many Parsis migrated to other parts of India. During the seventeenth century some of them went to the town of Navsari, 200 miles north of Bombay city, where, more than a century later, Nusserwanji Tata was born.

In his long span Nusserwanji survived many fluctuations of fortune. Apprenticed to a Hindu banker and merchant, the boy lived frugally, saved a small sum of money, branched out on his own, and by the time he was seventeen had established his own business and a family. Twenty years later his first and only son, Jamshedjee, took charge of extensive Tata trading with China and Japan through offices in Hongkong and Shanghai. The firm sold cotton and opium, and in return sent tea, silk, copper, and gold to India.

By the time he was twenty-six, Jamshedjee was already a rich man. When the following year the Civil War locked up American shipping and Indian cotton soared, like many other Bombay families the Tatas envisioned incredible prosperity ahead. Early in 1864 Jamshedjee Tata sailed for England with a fortune in bills of exchange on the Chinese markets. By the time he landed the cotton crash had made them quite worthless. Young Tata was not only no longer rich, he was broke and in debt. By retrenching and selling off large parcels of property, he and his father paid off the creditors in full and re-established the firm's credit.

The Tata fortunes then lay fallow for some years, until, in fact, the Emperor of Abyssinia imprisoned a few Britishers in a rather arbitrary fashion and General Sir Robert Napier, Commander-in-Chief of the troops in Bombay, was ordered to Africa to teach him a lesson. Nusserwanji Tata headed a group of Bombay merchants who supplied various commodities required for the soldiers. In the six months of that punitive campaign the Tatas and their associates netted a profit of one and a half million dollars.

During the time he spent in England after the crash, liquidating his consignments for whatever they would bring, Jamshedjee had toured the mills of Lancashire and had made a thorough study of cotton-goods production. It had struck him at the time that there was no reason why Indian cotton had to be woven in English mills. Why shouldn't Indians make their own yard goods? Now he took his share of the Abyssinian profits, formed a private company, and bought an old mill formerly used to press coconuts and castor beans for oil. He installed looms and spindles and became a cotton-cloth manufacturer—the first manufacturer in the history of the family. But almost immediately there were reports, known to a few in India, of new spindles in England and New England which would soon make his equipment obsolete. Luckily a syndicate of Bombay merchants bought the Alexandra mills at a profit and back he went to England.

The London of that day was a bustling, thriving metropolis, the clearing-house of the world's business. It was sensitive to the strengthening pulse of the fledgling countries of the United States and Germany. Jamshedjee met there men who were intimately concerned in the increasing prosperity of both lands as they grew out of agriculture and into industry.

There also, at a lecture in Manchester in 1867, Jamshedjee heard from his much-admired Thomas Carlyle the axiom, now well known, "The nation which gains control of iron soon acquires the control of gold". Iron! Why, thought the young Parsi, India is dotted with iron monuments which have withstood the elements for thousands of years, monuments demonstrating India's skill in iron-making before the first written history. If Germany and the United States were now able to contend with the great nations of the world because of their expanding iron industries, why couldn't India do the same? For the moment young Tata had to stick to his cotton business, but from then on he studied iron and steel methods at every opportunity and read everything written on the subject.

On the day when Queen Victoria was proclaimed Empress of India, January 1, 1877, Jamshedjee Tata opened his new mills in Nagpur, Central India. But his labourers were slow in adapting themselves to the new work, and in mistaken economy he had relied on cheap looms and spindles. Consequently his cloth was of poor quality and there wasn't much of it. The shares slumped. For a few years he struggled on, alone in his faith in his Empress mills. At Sunday morning gatherings at his home his friends and family indulgently let him talk of some day producing steel in India. Better to have him escape into daydreams than dwell on the very real difficulties at the cloth mills. In 1878 he saw the new English looms in operation in Manchester, threw out all equipment at the Empress mills, and started over again. During the following year the project paid 100 per cent dividends and the 1,000-rupee par value shares have stood between 10,000 and 15,000 for decades.

As we old-timers know, that scrapping Scot, Andrew Carnegie, got his nickname not from being pugnacious, but from his policy of scrapping all equipment, no matter how new and efficient, the moment newer machinery proved more economical. Whether Jamshedjee Tata absorbed that business philosophy from Carnegie or figured it out for himself, I don't know. But they both used the same method; they were both right.

With the spectacular success of the revitalized Empress mills, many wealthy Indians, formerly content with nominal returns from Government investments and who had been chary anyway of Indian projects, now sat at the Tata door in Bombay and begged Jamshedjee to invest their money in one of his enterprises. The house of Tata reopened offices in Shanghai and Yokohama, and new branches in Paris, London, and New York. Indian cotton, pearls from the Persian Gulf, drugs from China, all these passed through their hands. Jamshedjee Tata had the faculty of inspiring everyone who came into close contact with him.

Like B. P. Padshah. Padshah was an economics professor at Bombay University when Tata invited him to join the firm. Padshah accepted, but stipulated that he should receive no salary, nothing but his living expenses. He would devote his mind and energy to India, and therefore to the Tatas, because through them India would benefit economically.

Jamshedjee's son, Sir Dorab Tata, has told me a lot about his impressive father and the old man's well-tried devotion to the idea of steel made in India by Indians. Sir Dorab spent years of his youth in the Tata prospecting camps when Jamshedjee was looking for suitable deposits of iron ore. The Tatas were not, however, the first to work towards establishing a steel industry in India. In 1830, Josiah Marshall Heath, a retired Civil Service employee, obtained a grant from the East India Company and founded iron-works at Porto Novo, on the Madras coast, with furnaces capable of turning out about fifty tons of iron a week. His blowing engine was driven by bullocks! Several factors contributed to the failure of the Heath company: his British operators were inexpert, his iron ore fluctuated in quality, his costs were prohibitive, and he depended on charcoal as a fuel. Since he needed about four tons of charcoal to produce one ton of iron in those days, he soon ran out of charcoal. India, unlike the early American colonies, had few forests.

Then there was the Barakar Iron-Works, which commenced operations in 1875. The management benefited by Heath's experience with charcoal and located their plant on the Jherria coal-fields, 140 miles north-west of Calcutta. But their ore was poor, and four years later they closed their doors. Those same works were reopened later by the Indian Government as the Bengal Iron and Steel Company, and prospered until Martin and Company, Calcutta engineers in charge of the plant, went into steel production in 1905. After eight months they had to shut down. They had a good excuse. The pig-iron was found to have a high phosphorus content and the wear and tear on the furnaces in removing the phosphorus came high. I never understood, however, why they didn't look around for some ore with lower phosphorus percentage. If they had, they'd have found it less than 100 miles from Jherria, or about fifteen miles from our Noamundi fields. Now, after thirty-five years or so, having seen Tata's make a success of steel, they are back in production.

Strangely enough, the British, who are proverbially persistent, were easily discouraged from making steel in India. And yet it was not altogether strange, either, for they were still too close to the habits of thinking that produced the East India Company abuses. They lacked imagination. They did not foresee that they themselves were going desperately to need the very steel-making potentialities they were so sceptical about. They could not know that in 1919 Lord Chelmsford, then Viceroy, would say, "I can hardly imagine what we would have done if the Tata company had not given us steel for Mesopotamia, Egypt, Palestine, and East Africa". Also they were traders. They preferred to export steel *to* India, which they did—around a million and more tons a year—until 1914.

So when Jamshedjee Tata quietly started his search for an iron-ore body that would warrant the installation of a modern steel plant, the British paid little attention. Most of them felt, like the diehard fellows with me on the boat, that Indians were all right in their place, but steel-making was a cut above them. A big cut. A steel industry in India would not only compete with the English mills, but it wasn't practicable. Heath had proved that.

But men with a vision are stubborn. And Jamshedjee Tata had a vision. Armed with letters of introduction from Booth Tucker in London to two of his American friends, Tata sailed for the United States in 1892 in time for the World's Fair in Chicago. The two friends were George Westinghouse and Mark Hanna. The first was to be indirectly responsible for supplying hydroelectric power through hundreds of miles of Indian foothills to the Bombay Presidency. The second, when the time came, helped Jamshedjee Tata realize his vision.

Everywhere he went in America, Tata saw enough of the effects of the new steel industry on the life of the country itself to confirm him in the belief that if India, too, were to prosper it must produce steel. His son told me that the old man frequently referred to his favourite bit of American history to support this credo. Queen Elizabeth's Stuart successor, James I, stated in an edict that he noticed "with growing concern" the depletion of his New Forest from the inroads of charcoal-burners. Therefore, he said, he ordered the production of charcoal drastically curtailed. Immediately the colonists, who had plenty of charcoal for iron-making, increased the number and size of their blast furnaces, shipping iron to England to pay for imported commodities. Thus they gained not only national wealth and strength, but, possessing the vital material for defensive weapons, they felt a new measure of self-reliance. So that when George III and the Boston Tea Party came along, the colonists were able to produce some arms. Faced with war, American foundry owners limited production of shoes for oxen and worked overtime turning out swords and cannon. The Revolution might have had quite a different outcome had that Stuart loved his forests less.

Back in India during the next ten years Jamshedjee Tata employed an ever larger army of prospectors to scour the hills for iron and coal, in spite of the restrictive mining laws which tied up in endless governmental red tape any Indian who wanted to dig a hole in the ground. Finally, through Lord Curzon, the laws were relaxed somewhat in 1899. But time was slipping by the ageing Tata. Twenty years had passed since he had discovered the presence of metals in the Chanda district of Central India.

Jamshedjee determined to see Lord George Hamilton in London to get British approval of a pet project which would eventually promote the success of his bigger and principal enterprise—the putting aside some of the Tata millions to establish an Indian Institute of Science. Tata also wanted assurance that the money would be properly handled as long as the British remained in India.

Lord George Hamilton had been both Under-Secretary and Secretary of State for India. He was a great-hearted English gentleman, deeply concerned with Indian advancement. India has many reasons to be grateful to him, to Lord Curzon, Viceroy in Jamshedjee's time, and to perhaps the greatest of Viceroys, Lord Halifax. People who know and love India would like to feel that today all England's great men share the enlightened views of such men, and not those of Roberts and Kitchener, who advocated milking India dry.

Actually, it is only when one of the autocratic sort of Englishman gets into print that we realize that the spirit of the East India Company still lives, mouthing democracy as part of an empty ritual. Such a one was F. E. Smith, later Lord Birkenhead, who addressed the students of Oxford in 1927 in these words: "India is our prize possession. We in England have to live on it; the Indians may live in it. ... It is the task for you, the younger generation, to hold India to the last drop of your blood."

In London, after the details of the Institute had been settled, Lord George Hamilton was appalled at the manifold bureaucratic restrictions which had kept the Tata steel project back and promptly sent a letter to Lord Curzon. From that moment red tape fell away as if by magic, and Tata was free to apply for mining leases anywhere he pleased. Two years later he was even reproached for proceeding too slowly.

By the autumn of 1902 the groundwork had been done. Tata felt it was time to bring in American experts to co-ordinate what his experts had done, and to sift out the good deposits from the inferior. That sea journey to the United States undoubtedly seemed doubly long to the old man. He was not well; he knew he was soon to die. Neither ship nor train could keep pace with his impatient imagination and burning ambition.

Arriving at last in Cleveland, Jamshedjee Tata was variously described by the Press. One paper referred to him as "the J. P. Morgan of the East Indies". Another said that Li Hung Chang of China, then the richest man in the world, could hardly hope to sit in a poker game with him. Still another called him the "partner of the Nizam of Hyderabad". The Nizam of Hyderabad, by the way, was the Indian potentate who bought a dozen Rolls Royces some years ago, and then nearly had his chauffeur beheaded for daring to sit down in his presence to drive one of them !

The only welcome that interested Tata was that of his old friend, Mark Hanna. Hanna belonged to the most dynamic group of that generation of men who make today's giants seem to me like pygmies. He was a super-salesman. He thought big. He was big. Without a thought of profit to himself, Mark Hanna sold sixty million dollars' worth of American brains and equipment to the Tata family. Through him, Judge Elbert Gary had Tata meet many of the financiers and steel men of the day. Hanna saw to it that the largest steel plants were open to Tata and then took him to Washington to meet Julian Kennedy, at that time the leading steel-plant engineer of the world.

At a single gathering, Tata met and conferred with the Japanese and Chinese Ministers, the latter the great Wu Ting Fang; Elihu Root, then Secretary of War, Admiral George Dewey, fresh from Manila Bay, David B. Hill, First Assistant Secretary of State,

H. B. F. MacFarland, Commissioner of Washington, Dr. D. C. Gilman, president of the Carnegie Institute, and Colonel T. A. Bingham, representing President Roosevelt. And even in such a company Jamshedjee Tata impressed himself on the men he met. I have often heard it said that to meet him was to respect him. Ralph Watson, of the United States Steel Corporation, has told me that his eyes had a peculiar burning light, that he seemed to be bursting with pent-up energy.

Julian Kennedy was a practical man and an engineer. But he was not, and indeed could not have been, unmoved by the power of the dream that drove Jamshedjee Tata. "Produce the coal, the iron ore, and the limestone," said Kennedy as they parted, "give me the analysis, and I will build as large a plant as you desire, according to your own specifications, and so design it that it will be suited to the Indian climate."

So the designer of the plant was chosen, and Tata was one step nearer to his goal. Now he needed an expert to assemble the whole raw material set-up explored by his engineers. Kennedy suggested that Tata go and see Charles Page Perin. They had a strange, brief interview, those two men who were so different and were to work so closely together, in Perin's office in New York. I have the account from Perin himself.

"I was poring over some accounts in the office," he said, "when the door opened and a stranger in strange garb entered. He walked in, leaned over my desk, and looked at me for full a minute in silence. Finally he said in a deep voice, 'Are you Charles Page Perin?' I said yes.

"He stared at me again silently for a long time. Then slowly he said, 'I believe I have found the man I have been looking for Julian Kennedy of Pittsburgh has written you that I am going to build a steel plant in India. I want you to come to India with me, to find suitable iron ore and coking coal and the necessary fluxes. I want you to take charge as my consulting engineer. Mr. Kennedy will build the steel plant wherever you advise, and I will foot the bill. Will you come to India with me?'"

"What did you say?" I asked Perin. "That was a pretty quick decision to make."

"I was dumbfounded, naturally," Perin said, and then smile "But you don't know what character and force radiated from Tata's face. And kindliness, too. Well, I said yes, I'd go. And I did. But not just then. I sent my partner, Weld, over first scout the raw-materials situation."

That meeting, which was not without its own drama, is one of many refutations of Kipling's outworn negation—for the twain had met.

Jamshedjee Tata's visit to the United States took place during the most critical period of our labour-industry adjustment. Industrial demand had outstripped the labour market. At the wage rate paid by industrialists of the time, many Americans preferred long hours of farm work to long hours in a steel mill. Ten years before, the Homestead Strike, in protest against the current wage scale, had brought boatloads of European labour swarming up the Monongahela River and flooding into every mill town, imported by our own capitalists to "teach American labour a lesson". Not knowing the value of the dollar, and accustomed, besides, to even less pay in their old countries with their lower standards of living, the foreign labourers, most of them from Central Europe, lived on almost nothing and sent their savings back to their families.

But living on next to nothing meant existence in miserable, improvised wooden shacks, thrown up to house them. Since the newcomers seldom had families with them, one bedroom frequently accommodated four men, two on a day shift and two on the night. Sanitation was primitive, if there was any at all. Jamshedjee Tata saw these conditions, as I have myself, saw men sleeping in rooms warmed only by the heat of their unwashed bodies, rooms whose single windows were kept tightly shut to retain that meagre heat. These hovels were no credit to the country, and they furnished a vivid object lesson to the Parsi from the East. He determined to work his men no more than eight-hour shifts, and in a letter to his son, Dorab, in Bombay, he wrote: "Be sure to lay out wide streets planted with shade trees, every other one of a quick-growing variety. Be sure that there is plenty of space for lawns and gardens. Reserve large areas for football, hockey, and parks. Earmark areas for Hindu temples, Mohammedan mosques, and Christian churches."

Despite the care the Tatas took to create a plant-city of which they could be proud, where their workmen could live like human beings, some hovels did spring up around the town on land not owned by the company, to house the hangers-on and the gamblers, the rogues and the prostitutes. The same thing happened in one of the best-planned American steel towns, the Gary plant on Lake Michigan. But in both cases, as the city got over its growing pains, the slums disappeared.

Now that Indian and American enterprise and vision were joined, the Tata steel-mill project began to take definable shape. Perin's partner, Weld, had found the deposits of ore located by the prospectors to be of excellent quality but limited in quantity. Almost immediately, through a Bengali named P. N. Bose, Dorabjee Tata heard of a good iron-ore deposit Bose had noted some years before while working on a geological survey in the Drug district of Central India. Weld and a nephew of Jamshedjee's, Shapurji Saklatwalla, found the vein samples to run 67 per cent pure iron ! Close by, on Dhalli Hill, they found similar deposits.

The ore supply was assured. Coal was certainly going to come from the Jherria district of Bengal, about 500 miles away.

A steel plant, however, must be guaranteed a constant water supply. And, while in the United States you may have a pretty steady flow the year round, many Indian rivers dry up for a few months each year. A site was located on the Maheradi River about half-way between the ore deposits and the Bengal collieries. However, had this location been the final one chosen for the steel plant, the cost of hauling materials would have shut down the mills in a short time. But again Mr. Bose, like a sort of guardian angel, reported other ore deposits at Gurumaishini in the Mayurbhanj State in Orissa. By this time Charles Perin had arrived in India, and with Weld he tramped the Orissa hills during the hottest season of the year, finding at last a good quality of iron ore in apparently unlimited quantity, and much nearer the coal-fields. They picked the village of Sini for the site of the plant.

The set-up was nearly ideal: iron ore, coal, suitable fluxes (limestone, which is combined with silica and added to the ore) lay not far away, and confluent rivers seventy miles from the coal and fifty miles from the ore, on the Bengal Nagpur Railway—all the needed raw materials plus a water supply. Furthermore, the important port of Calcutta was only 150 miles away. The Tatas were now free to turn to the organization of a company to run the steel plant.

The magnitude of the financing involved in a rival enterprise kept out Indian competition for the time being. Also no competing firm could have effected the cheap assembly of raw materials so painstakingly worked out by the Tatas. In addition, the Tatas had the sympathy and encouragement of the Indian Government. But when they sought capital in London they were turned down cold.

Most English money barons of the time were still circumscribed by the tradition of the East India Company; none of them was especially interested in putting anything *into* India. Particularly did they look askance at floating any Indian project to be run by Indians. They had furnished money for South Sea speculations, for the Hudson's Bay Company, for opium trade with China, pearl fisheries in uncharted seas; but why, they reasoned, should they finance an Indian steel plant which would eventually shut off Indian steel markets from Sheffield and the Teesside ? After almost a year of negotiations in London, the Tatas saw that if they should raise any capital there, they would in time have to turn over the management to English control.

It was now the summer of 1907, and a new and powerful interior force was stirring the minds of the people of India, rich and poor alike, the Swadeshi movement. Swadeshi is roughly translated as "Produce your own goods".

Sir Dorab boldly decided to test his India, to see if it was possible to float the steel company in Bombay with Indian capital. The Britishers in India were complacent. Now you will see, they said wisely, how necessary it is to have England at your back with her money and brains. Indian capital, indeed!

The prospectus was issued in Bombay on August 27, 1907. And all through the day the Tata office was besieged by Indians, a few of whom were obviously opulent, but many of whom were dressed in the worn garments of the poor. They lined up in front of Navsari Mansions like Londoners waiting for first-night seats in the pit, some of them with stools and lunch boxes. The entire share capital was subscribed, in single shares or in blocks, by nearly 9,000 people in only eight days.

Later, when a bond issue for £400,000 was called for to provide working capital, the Maharaja Scindia of Gwalior took over the entire issue. This was a radical departure from custom, a tangible demonstration of the new spirit abroad in the land. Heretofore, Indian princes had hoarded their gold, and not only balked at investing it, but would have hesitated to involve it in any project of a fellow Indian.

The Indian railroads, more or less in the spirit of the London comedian who some years later offered to give £5,000 to the widow of the Unknown Soldier, agreed to purchase 20,000 tons of rails a year over a long period, provided, of course, that the rails passed the British Standard Specifications.

One more change took place before the ground was broken for the plant. It was brought about by an Irishman, and a colourful one at that, V. P. Piggott. Piggott's wealthy, landowning parents had sent him to India some time before hoping that the dry air would cure his ailing lungs. But when after a year he was still failing, he was sent on another trip, a long sea voyage to the Straits Settlements. Nobody, including his doctor, thought he would live to come back. But he did, and sixty pounds heavier from the diet of cod-liver oil and stout prescribed by the wise old captain of the boat. Not long after, Piggott heard about the proposed steel plant at Sini. Since his concern, the Midnapore Zemindary Company, owned vast tracts of land in that neighbourhood, he knew the terrain thoroughly.

Piggott took his own characteristic way of showing the Tatas a better location. Entraining three horses to be ready upon his arrival at the station of Kalimati, he sought out the Tata engineers at Sini. He was dressed in an old pair of khaki shorts and a mended khaki shirt and looked, as he said, "like a prospector or a loafer". After a considerable wait, Perin's men asked him into their tent and continued to sip long, cool whiskies without offering him one, an almost unforgivable insult in India. Hot and thirsty, Piggott took out his map, outlined the site he had in mind, and offered to take the two men there.

Once at Kalimati they mounted the waiting horses and rode to a magnificent spot on high, level ground, much nearer the ore-fields, where the Karkai could be seen flooding and tumbling into the Subarnarekha, which then flowed through a section almost devoid of rain. Tata's men immediately saw that the Subarnarekha, or Ribbon of Gold, was well named. It would have been only human if Piggott had shown some feeling of triumph, but he merely said quietly that if the engineers wanted the land, he would see that they got it, then produced an excellent lunch—with plenty of cooling drinks. For many of my years in India I lived in a bungalow built on the site of that luncheon.

Within a few weeks of Piggott's expedition, twenty-five square miles had been acquired on leaseholds at five rupees, or a dollar and a quarter, an acre around Sakchi, now called Jamshedpur (*pur* means town, so—Jamshed's town). Soon Pittsburgh mill were fabricating the blast furnaces and mill buildings, the scrub forest was disappearing at the hands of one band of engineers while another dammed the river, and the Bengal Nagpur Railway built a three-mile spur to the works and laid a new road, fifty miles long, to the Gurumaishini ore-bodies.

The work did not proceed without incident, and of a kind probably peculiar to India. The local tigers became enraged at the destruction of their forest homes and killed two of the aborigine An elephant, driven frantic by the disturbance and the noise smashed to powder a number of huts near the dam. One night a she bear entered the hut used as an office for the railway traffic department and cubbed under the superintendent's tab.

But even after the jungle hazards were overcome, the founding of Sakchi was not uncomplicated. Once cholera swept the works and the aborigines scattered to the surrounding hills. Newcomers brought malaria with them, and again many workers left overnight. Although one of the first buildings erected was a hospital, the little natives would not go there voluntarily. The men from up-country and the Bengalis did. A Santali girl, working in the brick department, had the first Tata Steel baby. While carrying a load of bricks on her head to the men in the recuperative chambers of the first open-hearth furnace, she felt her time coming and she was delivered in the checker chamber. What's more, when the baby was born, she picked it up and walked off to her home with it.

The original plant Julian Kennedy had been commissioned to design and build for the Tatas consisted of two blast furnaces, four open-hearth furnaces, a rail and structural mill, and a small bar mill. Also coke-ovens to supply the blast furnaces. The blast furnaces were guaranteed to produce 175 tons a day—they soon averaged 250 tons a day. In 1942 the first one of these furnaces was removed to make room for a new one of 1,000-ton capacity. The demolition engineers were amazed at the condition of the old furnace. Every rivet was as tight as the day it was driven; hardly any corrosion was visible. The Kennedy open-hearth furnaces still produce steel economically, although now enlarged and implemented along more modern lines. The Kennedy rolling-mills remain and can function perfectly, even though more up-to-date mills have for some time been handling the total output of the plant. Somehow or other we have been loath to level those old mills.

I have a warm spot in my heart for them. They remind me of the days when we rolled rails and six-inch rounds for the Allies. I think of the days when the Britishers working in the plant reported calmly at their jobs as usual, the death notice of a soldier brother or son in their pockets. I think of the Christmas dance at the Institute in 1916, when the British couples danced the Lancers.

The most serene of the women fainted as the dance ended. In her bag was a letter saying that her brother's body had been blown to bits in France.

I remember, too, later that same Christmas night, old John the Welshman sitting in the coke-oven office, his head buried in his hands. I knocked at the door, and after a bit he welcomed me in with a handshake and a Merry Christmas and poured tea for me. I asked him, "What news from home this week?"

"They bloody well got the fourth lad," he answered slowly. "At least the missus got his tag back." Then, after a pause, "I've just written and told her to get the youngster ready. He's almost seventeen now and big for his age. She'll send him over like the rest of them. We're going to win this bloody war yet."

Those old steam-driven rolling mills are part of all that, of all the good things and the hard times, too, that have gone towards making the Tata plant what it is. And what they didn't take part in themselves, they saw from the sidelines, like the honoured pensioners they are. Now there's another war and work for them to do. It's a safe bet they're doing it as well as They always did.

CHAPTER III

RACING IS GOOD FOR THE LIVER

Before the plant site had been selected, before the organization which was to run the steel mill had been formulated, even before the coke and ore veins had been located, Jamshedjee Tata had, in letters from America to his son, outlined the proposed personnel of the plant.

From what he had seen of steel plants in the United States, he wrote, Tata's must have American management; the Welsh seemed best fitted to carry out the coke-oven installations; Americans were leading the world in blast-furnace production; the Germans showed superior skill in producing open-hearth feel; and the British were still ahead of the others in rolling-mill practice. Although the old man died in Badnauheim in 1904, that was the set-up I found operating when I went to work for Tata's nine years later.

Three large bungalows had been built next each other in Jamshedpur to house the bachelors. These were called chummeries. The married couples had their own comfortable houses of the same general type. One chummery was allotted to the Americans, one to the Germans, and the third to the English and the Welsh. Fifteen dollars a month were paid for room rent and food, and another five dollars secured the services of a personal servant. We bought whisky in six-gallon lots at wholesale prices and divided it four ways. That made it come to about eighty-five cents a quart.

This scale of living opened a new and rosy vista to the blast-furnace boys from eastern Pennsylvania. If they'd been a little more abstemious, they could have saved two-thirds of their pay. And some of them did. But many of the lads could not stand prosperity. They got homesick. They drank more than their health could stand. Gradually they drifted back to the States. But on the whole they did what they had been brought out to do: they trained Indians in blast-furnace operation. The native boys learned how to make pig-beds and to lead the molten iron into them, where, from its shape and colour, it is called the sow. Branching out at right angles from the sow a number of troughs about a yard long drain off the liquid metal. These troughs form what are called pigs. The Indians quickly learned to break off the pigs while they were still hot. In fact, they acquired all the knowledge which is needed to run a blast furnace skilfully.

The British crowd who came out to run the rolling-mills were all experienced men who had worked in mills identical with the ones Tata's was building. But the rolling-mills were not ready for full-out operation for some two years after the Britishers got there. During the two years, while those men reported for work every day, they were quite often sent home again, since there was no steel to roll. But they were stolid individuals. They drank their ale and beer conscientiously, much as they would have taken medicine. Less phlegmatic people would have had at least some casualties in D.T.'s from the enforced idleness, the low cost of liquor, and the enervating climate.

While there was no discrimination in Tata minds between nationalities, or even for that matter between castes and creeds, certain marked national differences were there. Some of them showed up immediately; some of them we discovered only after the first World War began.

The German open-hearth expert who had recruited the men for his department filled out his crew with as fine a group of heavy-drinking, brawling scum of the earth as were ever gathered together to run a steel plant. His mind ran to Prussian guards as the American expert's favoured relatives of All-American football players. For one key position the German picked out a man who had had no steel-making experience at all; he had, however, been an officer in the Kaiser's own regiment.

The one thing that all the Germans at Tata's had in common was that they were certainly not immoral. They were simply unmoral. They even bragged about it.

There was the German in a neighbouring bungalow who was so soft-hearted he wept when he listened to records of the opera *Martha*. He had a dog named Askim, of which he was very fond. One night when Askim returned from one of his periodic absences, the German started to pat him and then, in an access of rage, grabbed the dog by the hind legs and smashed his brains out on the concrete veranda post. I think the man was just lachrymose, because he wept over the loss of his pet, too.

One of our German workmen and his wife boarded a baker's dozen of other Germans. Not only did the husband have to go to Calcutta for treatment of a virulent syphilitic infection, but so, one by one, did all the boarders. This was an extreme, but not an unusual, case.

The German contingent seemed to be proud, too, of one hell of a row they made in the bungalow of a sullen Austrian couple who furnished meals to a lot of them. It was over some order from Bob Wells, the general manager, which they resented, I forget now just what. Anyway, they all foregathered there, drinking, shouting threats, and planning to take over the company for themselves. Bob Wells was just out of the hospital and was as weak as a kitten, but he thought he ought to go in there and bring them to their senses.

He got together a couple of Bengal-Nagpur Railway men who subsequently disappeared when the going got rough, and T. W. Tutwiler, who was foreman of blast furnaces and a good man in a tight spot. They had no more than entered the place when the Austrian woman put out the lights, evidently by prearrangement, and the Germans closed in on the two American Tata officials with their fists and anything else handy. Finally Tut managed to get Wells and himself out on the veranda, sent Wells off, and backed up against the wall, where he took all comers. Somehow the bottles hurled at him missed, and by the time he left there were a lot of chastened German open-hearth men thinking things over.

After the plant had got into operation the German crews claimed that the pig-iron produced by our blast furnaces was chemically out of order. Since they couldn't use it and India required only a small amount, large piles of pig accumulated around the furnaces. When I landed in India in June of 1913, there were 95,000 tons of pig-iron in stock, and I don't know how much more had piled up when the war broke out. Then it was sold at a fancy price, mostly to Japan.

With the stock pile constantly on the increase because the Germans could not or would not make steel, the company's shares dropped to the cellar. Once I heard a Parsi in the accounting department trying to induce some of the American boys to buy shares, then at less than a third of their par value. He was laughed at. In 1918 those shares, which had been as low as 10, hit 1,900 in the Bombay Stock Exchange, and paid a dividend of over sixty rupees per share. Had those men from the States had enough confidence in their own ability and faith in the company to have invested even one month's pay in Tata stock, they would have cleaned up a profit of more than $54,000, besides collecting huge dividends. When I left India in 1941 an old friend gave me a bottle of 1875 brandy. Across the label he wrote, "To be opened when deferred shares hit 5,000". I shall be surprised if the cork remains in the bottle much longer.

Even though the German-run open-hearth furnaces were not producing steel, some of the rolling-mills were soon ready. In 1912 a batch of rail-steel ingots imported from England were rolled on the bloomer and rail mills into finished rails. I have a slice of the first rail rolled on that 18th of March. It makes a fine paper-weight.

But the Germans continued to find our pig-iron unsuitable for their furnaces, and by the next spring many Indians were convinced that out attempt to produce steel on a commercial basis was bound to fail. The stockholders began to grumble. The British had tried twice to make steel in India and failed, they said, and if the German steel masters couldn't produce open-hearth stuff, no one could. Then the Germans, jealous of their reputation, went to work to find and correct the trouble. The only thing was that they refrained from taking the company fully into their confidence.

They found that moisture was penetrating into the underground flues and recuperative chambers, so that the furnaces could not retain temperatures high enough to produce good steel. That much we all learned. They decided to surround the underground chambers and flues with a tunnel. The moisture would then seep into the tunnel and be carried away. But only the Germans knew of the tunnel. It was driven secretly, without blueprints. When that part of the excavation was finished which encompassed the furnaces like a moat, another tunnel was started to connect with the first and lead any water away to escape through the slag dump.

About this time a German sausage-maker from Calcutta, "Guts" Myers, commenced paying weekly visits to Jamshedpur. He used to get together with the Germans working at Tata's for lengthy evening conferences—always behind closed doors. Nobody in India at that time had any thought of there being a war. But that sausage-maker must have known something was going to happen. He told his compatriots that India must not produce steel yet, not, indeed, until India had become a colony of the great and glorious German Empire.

The work on the tunnel stopped abruptly. With, in fact, so much haste and secrecy that scaffolds, electric wiring, trowels, and cement containers were left inside and the manholes and the entrances sealed over. The ground level was even raised a few feet to conceal the manholes.

But now the plotters had something else to worry about. The company had cabled Charles Page Perin to come to India and prove that he could make steel in the plant. When the Germans heard about it Perin was already on the seas, bringing with him a young open-hearth man from Pittsburgh, Ralph Watson, now vice-president of U.S. Steel, then loaned to Perin by the Carnegie Steel Company. Watson had picked out a German-American of experience to go along, a man who spoke only German during his stay in Jamshedpur. But the German contingent did not take Watson's assistant into their confidence. They hoped that by keeping the existence of the tunnel to themselves and waiting until the American consultants had gone again, the company could be convinced that their steel project was doomed.

Still, no amount of Germanic wishful thinking could prevent the tunnel from doing just what it was intended to do. The moisture which had kept down the temperatures of the furnaces obediently trickled into the underground ditch, condensed there, and ran out into the ground, far away from the furnaces.

Ralph Watson, however, knew his business. He sent the German superintendent home and put Lansing Hoyt from Evanston in his place. Together the two men took over. Before half a year had passed, the open-hearth department had produced 8,000 tons of steel in one month.

Now the Germans saw the game was up. They couldn't fool Ralph Watson. And it would be a reflection on their nationality and their skill if they were replaced by Americans. They turned to and produced steel.

One evening during the months before the war I had happened on some indication of "Guts" Myers' activities when I dropped into the bungalow of my next-door neighbour, also a German. It had been a hot day, with the thermometer at 120, and I couldn't sleep. There were some thirty Germans sitting about drinking beer and listening to "Guts", who harangued them in grand style. He quieted down when I came in and offered me a bottle of Munich beer which had been chilled in a bath-tub filled with ice and water.

"It's a new religion I am telling them about," he said smoothly, "the Brotherhood of Man."

After the crowd had left, my neighbour revealed that the oration had concerned the awakening of Germany, the day when the Kaiser would rule the world. "The Kaiser is crazy," he said. "Still, if Germany can get her food, she can beat the world."

He didn't tell me, however, of the tunnel. That secret was well kept; it wasn't discovered until 1922, when another man and I stumbled on it one day quite by accident.

I met "Guts", the sausage-maker, again three years after that discovery on an Italian liner between Cairo and Venice. Our old Swiss engineer, Ernest Blaser, was along too. "Guts" recognized him, but remembered me only as the man who had backed a horse from 15 to 1 to off the books at Lucknow in the Civil Service Cup some years before. He tried to sell me an estate in Switzerland for $200,000, dirt cheap at the price, he said. And it looked it from the photographs, which showed endless beautiful lawns, a lake, and a real castle at the top of a hill. Later, when he was drunk, he admitted to Blaser that he had bought the place in 1918 as a refuge for the Kaiser. But the Kaiser had preferred Doorn, and now poor "Guts" was stuck with the estate. I didn't relieve him of it.

The sausage-maker wasn't around in 1914 when the war started, so he escaped being interned with the rest of the Germans, who were sent to Ahmednagar, on the west coast of India. The British camp guards there were very lenient with their prisoners. They winked at the rule confining them to bounds and let many of them get out for a while and enjoy themselves, sometimes even joining them for a few at the local pub. Those guards knew little about the war. Most of them had never been under fire.

In the autumn of 1914, however, what was left of a regiment which had been in the Marne retreat was shipped out to India and took over as guards at Ahmednagar. Those boys had been through hell. They had a healthy hatred for any member of the nation which had perpetrated the atrocities they had seen during that retreat. My former next-door neighbour, the German, one day disregarded a sentry's order to return to camp where he belonged.

He laughed at the soldier and called him an English son-of-a-bitch. He was shot dead in his tracks.

A great many men today, especially Indians, think that we Americans who were in the country at that time exaggerate the German activities in India. They scoff at talk of sabotage. Those men are like that first lot of camp guards; they just haven't been through it. They weren't in Jamshedpur when, within an hour after we heard of the declaration of war, the Germans held a secret meeting and then refused in a body to make munitions for use against the Fatherland. The sceptics didn't see T. W. Tutwiler, who had recently been made general manager, call on the Government for militia to keep them at work until the new technicians could arrive from America.

Tutwiler posted militia guardsmen armed with guns and with bayonets on the ready around every job which employed Germans, to prevent sabotage and to keep them producing. For three weeks he slept at the plant, constantly making the rounds himself. If there'd been a less aggressive, less intelligent man in his place, the plant would have slowed down, the open-hearth furnaces would have cooled off and died, and we would have been months getting into production again.

During the two decades after the first World War some Indian patriots and business men flirted with what is called the "New Germany", not realizing that in exchange for India's gold Germany had only a mess of pottage to offer. Britain has chained the country, but the chains have been bearable and are being steadily loosened. Germany would tighten the chains and add the whip.

That same old Swiss engineer, Ernest Blaser, who was on the boat trip from Cairo to Venice when we met "Guts" Myers, had a fund of homely platitudes. He was a sweet old man, who lumbered along on flat feet in size twelves. We used to tease him about his sayings. But the trouble with platitudes is that usually they're right. So was old Blaser. We raised hell with him once because the three boiler plants under his care were not producing the quantity of steam needed to operate the plant at maximum capacity. We knew that a lot of the coal we had sent him was pretty rotten, but we didn't tell him that. Finally, he said, "My boilers are in good condition. You tell me the coal is good. It looks good. It should produce plenty of steam. You can fool me. But you can't fool the boilers. Looks are often deceptive."

Two of my best friends in India were like that. They looked like fops. They were both majors in the British Army. Nobby and Gin Bill they were. Nobby was a clean-cut-looking officer with a good brain. But he affected a monocle and collected goldfish. He also carried a swagger stick. I dropped into Nobby's quarters for a cocktail one evening while he was still dressing. His monocle was lying on the dresser. The eye customarily held open by the monocle was merely a closed slit. Nobby had left that eye somewhere along the Marne. The monocle camouflaged the glass fake which replaced it when Nobby was "dressed".

The other major bloke, nicknamed Gin Bill, was a fine fellow and a tough soldier. He had been smeared up so often in France that some superior had pushed him off to Mesopotamia to get a rest. He landed in Mesopotamia just in time to be in Kut during the siege. After the war, Bill waged two battles with the D.T.'s. He won both fights. Many of his friends claimed he had no right to be alive.

Gin Bill dropped in to lunch one day. Although he ate sparingly, he did pretty well for a fellow who religiously followed a liquid diet. All went fine until the meat course arrived with poached eggs on top, like a golden buck. Gin Bill turned green and left the table. Later that day I met him at the club and he explained. It seemed that that morning Bill had awakened in his usual state as a result of mixing brandy with too many gins the night before. He had told his bearer to bring him a prairie oyster. The bearer had failed to notice the advanced state of development of the egg and Bill had swallowed it and its accompaniment of Worcester sauce before *he* noticed it. The odds, as Gin Bill computed them, were something like this: about three to one that he would need a prairie oyster; about three thousand to one that the bearer wouldn't observe the condition of the egg. That made it a nine-thousand-to-one shot that he would get a soothing potion for his nerve-racked stomach. In addition, the odds were about ten thousand to one that there would be poached eggs for lunch.

"Figure it out for yourself," he said. Mathematically it works out to around a ten-million-to-one shot. "But can I ever pick a winner at any odds?" he complained. "I cannot. Racing, boxing, or football, I pick the loser."

With all his toughness as a seasoned soldier, Bill was a hero-worshipper. He idolized Napoleon and Sir Hector MacDonald. Bill talked a lot about fighting, and he always came back to MacDonald's feats in South Africa under Roberts and Kitchener, to one exploit in particular. Arriving at an objective after a three day forced march, MacDonald was asked by the commander how soon his men would be ready to go in. MacDonald faced his men and barked, "Fall in !" Turning back to the commander, MacDonald said, "My men are ready to attack upon word from you".

As Bill put it, "The commander did, MacDonald did, and the men did".

Neither Nobby nor Bill believed the story that MacDonald had committed suicide in Paris. Both claimed he had simply dropped out of sight, to turn up later as a leader of the White Russians under a different name.

Gin Bill knew a thing or two about golf. We all felt that he could have been the greatest golfer of all time if he had ever taken the time to play a few sober holes. Players who talk about lakes, trees, and man-made hazards on ordinary courses should play a few rounds on the Jamshedpur course.

The player tees up and sees a long sloping fairway with the first hole 400 yards off. About 100 yards ahead on the left, he sees an old temple, "half as old as time", well walled in and shaded by green trees. Any ball landing in the temple grounds is out of bounds, and the old priest makes plenty of coppers selling almost new balls to players. If our man hits the ball straight, he can know he is well away. But if he slices, his ball will find an old sunken road running downhill, worn out of the earth by the passage of countless bare and calloused feet.

The sixth hole was rightly called the topper's delight. During the hot season the fairway baked harder than a bookmaker's heart. Five hundred and fifty yards long, and slightly downhill, you could let yourself go and lay against the ball. If you hit it straight you had a chance of picking up a four or even a two. And if you did, you bought drinks for the crowd at the clubhouse. That was the written rule; so called because the bar boys used to get writer's cramp making out chits.

I have seen some great performances on that course, besides having made a donkey of myself there many a time. A High Court judge, formerly a coxswain at Oxford, played every shot with rhythm and co-ordination. The only men who could beat him regularly were the caddy master and Gin Bill. That caddy master couldn't read or write. He belonged to one of the backward tribes of the local hills and at first could speak only in the Kohl dialect. Someone gave him an old mashie and a worn-out ball. As he walked about the course picking up stones or blades of long grass, he would knock the ball around. In no time at all he blossomed out as an instructor. That boy was the greatest and most natural golfer any of us had ever seen; before he was sixteen he averaged 68 for five rounds, on that course. And he came from a "backward" tribe.

Gin Bill once turned in a performance that is worth mentioning. He played over nine holes one day before lunch and chalked up a 34. At lunch he folded in half a dozen gin and bitters to start and followed with three large bottles of heavy beer. It was a torrid day. Usually Bill's drive was the golfer's sweetheart, long and straight, with a gradual rise at about 100 yards. But after lunch he couldn't tee up his ball. The caddy master did it for him. After three mighty swipes at the ball, Bill hit it straight down the fairway for 300 yards. Later he drove off a short hole—a 165-yard affair—with a mashie-niblick and landed the ball on the rim of the cup. In short, he finished the nine holes with a score of 39. Taking his luncheon diet and the weather into consideration, that round was the greatest I have ever seen.

Between the time that a man ends his game of golf and the coming of darkness in India is only the wink of an eye. Violet Malcolm, under her pen name of Laurence Hope, wrote:

The night falls swiftly; this sudden land
Can never lend us a twilight strand
'Twixt the daylight shore and the ocean night,
But takes—as it gives—at once, the light.

We who have lived in India have all felt those moments, when the mist which has gathered on the lower rice paddies eddies and swirls uphill, overflowing the sunken road and spilling out and up. Sitting on the porch with Gin Bill, I have watched the Santalis, or coolies, men and women, surge down the road, singing as they went, after the day's toil. The fog covered their legs, they looked to be wading in a soft white river. Now they were covered to the hips, now their backs and well-rounded breasts gradually disappeared into the mist and were lost to view. Only the unison of their voices remained to tell of their passing. Then silence, broken now and then by the thin tinkle of the temple bells, and the whir of the flying fox wheeling about overhead.

After a few drinks Gin Bill would tell tales of the border lands where he had seen duty, pursuing raiders through rugged mountain passes where any rock might conceal a lurking rifleman, where men recognized no law but that of self-preservation.

Bill seemed as interested in the steel works at Jamshedpur as in stories of fighting brigands in the Afridi country. But the magnitude of the mills and the furnaces was too much for him. With no head for figures, Bill could not bring himself to believe that sixty-five miles of railroad functioned inside that steel plant, that twenty-seven locomotives worked day and night hauling cars of raw materials to the various departments and carrying away finished steel ready for shipment. A million soldiers, yes, Bill could understand such a figure. But that Tata's consumed a million and a half tons of coal a year, and required two millions tons of iron ore yearly to keep the blast furnaces and steel works running full, simply made him throw up his hands and say he was only a country boy, after all. He never could believe that a huge industrial plant and the large modern city surrounding it could have been dropped down in the heart of an Indian jungle.

And the jungle presses close about Jamshedpur. Travel five miles out of the city in any direction and you are in the jungle, in old India. Within the town there are the picture-houses, the clubs, the radio at your elbow, with perhaps a running commentary on the Derby or a political convention in the States. But such Western innovations are, after all, surface things. There are constant reminders of the teeming, untamable life of India all about, unseen, sometimes intangible, but strongly felt.

On my first evening in my bungalow in Jamshedpur I killed a scorpion on the front veranda. That night a mare foaled not ten yards from my bedroom window. I took that last as an omen. During succeeding years I owned many horses, racers; some of them good, some not. And luckily I managed to keep pretty well in the black.

Tata's furnish playing-fields, tennis-courts, and a large Institute, not unlike the Y.M.C.A., for the use of their employees. But I believe they are unique in having laid out a race-track, paddocks, stables, a grandstand, bar, and betting ring for their workmen. But that race-course turned a crowd of nostalgic foreigners, counting their remaining days in India, into a contented lot of workmen who did more and better work and signed on time after time for further periods. Before the company created the race-course in 1913 the labourers complained that they had no recreation except walking—and that walk usually led to a bar. In the two years after the start of operations in 1911 more foreigners were fired and sent home than were discharged during the following twenty years.

In the tropics, a man's temperament and efficiency depend a good deal on the state of his liver. Riding a horse is one of the best ways to keep the liver in order. Almost any man will refuse to buy a horse as a purely therapeutic measure, but if he has a course where he can have a gallop and feel that exhilaration which comes from real riding, he has an incentive. Then you have a "gentleman rider" and a fit workman. As soon as our first race-track was laid out, it seemed as though every European in the place owned a horse. They rode to work followed by their grooms. In the afternoon the horses were brought to the gates, the men climbed aboard and went off to bathe and change and set out for the track for a gallop. Many a race-horse owner started out with one moke, only to find himself in a short time running a small racing stable with his own colours.

Pat, the stableman, was the one who turned us into racing riders. He was a gnarled ex-cavalryman with appropriately bowed legs, and a relentless drill-master. His skin looked scrofulous, the after-effect of a camel bite. After Pat had taught us greenhorns to saddle up and to sit a proper seat, he took us out on a football field, made us learn to trot and canter. Then he took away our stirrups and the fun commenced. Every day a few of us would come a cropper. Pat would be there before we could do more than pick ourselves up. With a fairly good imitation of a hungry tiger, Pat would snarl, "Who gave you permission to dismount?"

A few months more of schooling and we were made to ride without touching our bridles.

An adjutant of the district's mounted militia, known as the Chota Nagpur Light Horse, was greatly impressed with Pat's raw recruits. He saw to it that we had a sizable troop of light horse in town with the Government supplying some sixty additional mounts. I believe that second batch of horses cost us four dollars apiece. The Government paid allowances for fodder and furnished free army saddles to any man who put in two hours' drill a week. This encouragement fired Pat's ambition in earnest. He started an honest-to-God riding-school on the fallow rice-fields.

Rice-fields are inseparable from one's mental picture of India. On the plains where the ground is more or less level, large areas are divided into small plots by mud and sod bunkers. Water comes from adjacent ponds or rivers.

In rolling terrain, where lakes or rivers are few, the ancient aboriginal tribes had to build lakes or encatchment basins, usually on high ground. Rice grows under water, and the rainy season lasts only from June until September, while the harvest is gathered in October. Mud dams on high points of land empound water during the monsoons and ensure the paddy-fields from drying up, for when rain is scarce the natives open sluice-gates in the upper tanks and let the water flow from one terraced field to the succeeding fields below.

After the harvest, paddy-fields are allowed to remain fallow for a while and cows and buffalo are turned in to graze on the stubble. Pat picked one of those paddy areas, an extremely hilly one, on which to train us in jumping during the cold season. The horses loved it from the first, and after we stopped falling off we did too. We'd start at the bottom of the hill, jump the dams all the way up, then turn round and gallop down again.

The natives quite rightly resented our trespassing. Often we would stampede their cattle. If some water buffalo were mixed in with the herd, however, it was usually they who ran us to cover, the villagers laughing and shouting and egging on their champions.

Three men were concerned in the laying out of the track in Jamshedpur: a police sergeant who later became a major in the army, a cavalryman who had seen service in South Africa with Roberts, and a fine old ex-cavalry officer from the Indian Army who spoke with a smooth west-country Irish brogue. These three put their proposition up to Bob Wells, who was then general manager, and Bob thought it sounded good. True enough, the men might fall off their horses and break their necks, but that would be pleasanter than dying from delirium tremens. He told the trio to lay out the course, and when a racing club had been formed he would furnish material for fences, grandstands, and stables. Then the club could repay the company out of proceeds. As a matter of fact, the company later nullified the debt.

Some sixty men became charter members of a Gymkhana Club, with eighteen agreeing to buy mounts. The policeman and ex-cavalryman were elected to design and construct the course. They decided on a tricky four-furlong track shaped like a question mark with the top straight. Those boys knew a bit about racing. They made the run from the four-furlong post on the outside to the furlong post at the bend on the inside just fourteen yards shorter than from the four-furlong post on the inside rail to the bend. Whenever either happened to be riding, the other would always act as starter. The rider would ask permission to take his horse to the outside, claiming that his mount was fractious. Permission was always given. The other riders didn't complain, since they thought he was penalizing his horse. The flag would drop, and off would go the outside horse on a straight line for the rail on the bend, thereby gaining a clear fourteen yards. Those two gentlemen riders kept that secret for two years.

As soon as a betting ring, paddock, and bar were built, several boxes of horses arrived and the boys had something to think about besides going home. Their consumption of liquor dropped, their livers subsided, and their spirits rose. Immediately mill production soared. Men who had been working twenty days in the month began putting in full time. Sunday racing in Jamshedpur was in.

After the start of the war, when the German workers were replaced by British and American steel men, we thought the interest in racing would increase. We were badly mistaken. Only a few of the English newcomers took more than a passing interest. They claimed that the bookmakers cramped the odds, our horses were no good, our riding was hopeless, and our track was a joke. They were homesick for England and the English tracks with the milling crowds and dozens of bookies shouting, "Prices!".

During the cold-weather months those Britishers started a week-end exodus for Calcutta, where they could see real racing. They either knew or made friends with the English jockeys, and it was a little like being home again. But these friendships weren't too good for the mills. For the jockeys would give their new pals good tips. And when time came for the train to leave for Jamshedpur, our British workmen were celebrating, spending their winnings on endless toasts to the boys at home fighting the war. They were good for the night. The next morning, Sunday, they would have a few more to the boys over there, and start all over again. Even if they caught the mail train back that night, they were seldom fit for work Monday morning or even sometimes on Tuesday. In the meantime the furnaces were being operated without them, probably by men of less experience. At this time, when the furnaces were being pushed to the limit to supply the Allies with shells and rails, it was a serious matter.

The war-time general manager, T. W. Tutwiler, we alternately called King Tut and Old Tut, depending on whether he had just bawled us out as only he could, or we were admiring his two-fisted, bull-necked efficiency at getting a very tough job done, and done right. Old Tut, then, knowing that if he could keep the men in town over the week-ends he could increase production volume, decided to interest outside owners and to build a real track, a six-furlong job, with bars, tea-room, grandstand, and betting ring. The whole project was completed and the first race meeting held within two months. The railroad ran special trains from Calcutta right to the track. Tutwiler persuaded some of the smaller Calcutta owners to send up sixty-odd horses. Eight races were run on the first of a five-day meeting, four Sundays and Christmas Day. Half a dozen of Calcutta's biggest bookmakers stood up to be fired at by the country boys. Maurice Hallett, deputy commissioner in the Indian Civil Service, put his stamp of approval on Sunday racing by allowing his wife to present the cups. Besides the huge local attendance, a large group of people came up from Calcutta to see the fun.

When we laid out the track we had only one idea in mind, to keep our men at home so the mills could run full out. We hadn't given a thought to the effect our meetings might have on the bureaucratic autocrats who ran the Calcutta track. But a clergyman, speaking from a Calcutta pulpit, charged that we were defiling the Sabbath, and the descendants of the East India Company took up the chorus.

Few of the Calcutta racing men were within range of the preacher's voice during that sermon. Some of them were clocking their horses, some were playing golf, some were sitting around their clubs drinking up gin and bitters. But they called a meeting to devise a way of stopping the sacrilegious Sunday racing, and, incidentally, to prevent the exodus of horses which should instead be running on their track. They passed a new mandate threatening with disbarment any bookmaker, jockey, or trainer who supported any race meeting not under the organized rules of racing. Those rules were also, as a matter of fact, of their own making. They were clever enough not to mention Sunday racing. The smaller owners from Calcutta promptly withdrew from our project, all but one, J. C. Galstann, probably the most picturesque figure of any race-track.

His support alone went a long way towards keeping racing alive in Jamshedpur, keeping the men in town, and keeping the tonnages high.

Our British steel-workers vowed they would never again set foot on a Calcutta track, and offered to work on Sundays just as on week-days. That arrangement boosted production 20 per cent. And we still had our race meetings. Old J. C. Galstann would send up a dozen horses with a note telling us to enter, run, or scratch them all at our own discretion. He paid all expenses, and they were not small. He had already turned over his Calcutta mansion to the Government for a military hospital, but with his race-horses he helped indirectly towards making munitions.

Galstann had passed the three-score mark, but he could take fences with the best of them, and as for betting, he once laid £40,000 to win £25,000. He had started his career as a newsboy in Calcutta at the age of seven. When I knew him he practically controlled the lac market of the world, and lac is needed for varnishing windings for cannon. Most of the good stories about racing in India involve old J. C. somehow. For instance, the Calcutta handicapper was a pompous fellow who from time to time allotted weights that irked old J. C. Once Galstann entered a new horse in a six-furlong race for weeds. The new horse looked to be rather big for racing, and was certainly not in racing form. The handicapper's odds were rather short against him. When the entries reached the starting gate, one well-known bookmaker laid ten thousand to one that Galstann's horse would not run one, two, three.

The stewards smelled a rat, and the pompous handicapper went red and began to sweat, realizing that his leg was being pulled. The starting gate went up and all the horses galloped away. All of them except Galstann's nag, which got away with the rest of the field and then proceeded along the course at the only gait he knew. In fine form, he trotted slowly around the course and finished three furlongs behind the field, while the crowds rocked with laughter and the handicapper looked ready for apoplexy. Galstann's groom, waiting for the horse, removed the saddle, put on its usual gear, backed it into Galstann's carriage shafts, and stood ready to take the owner home.

There's another one about the time when J. C. rode one of his horses, Pier, at the Barrackpore track. J. C. was then past sixty. But he drove his mount up to dead-heat with another entry, Quality II. Both Pier and Galstann were fairly done up at the end of the race. Still, when the owner of Quality II voted to run off the dead-heat, the old man had to comply, except that he put another rider on Pier. He picked out a raw Australian lad, just off a boat with a load of remounts, and told him to use his own discretion, but not to hurt his mount, which was wet-coated and seemed to be fractious. The other owner issued the same instructions. He then backed J. C.'s horse off the books, which meant that Galstann couldn't put up a bean on the race.

I got the story from the jockey on Quality II, who later rode for me. The two horses got to the post and the gate went up. But both mounts stood still. The Australian jockey told the starter to go to blazes, that Pier wouldn't start until Quality II did. Finally Quality II jumped off and Pier followed at a canter. Quality II won by half a furlong. Pier kept right on going and was finally pulled up on the opposite side of the track. The Australian dismounted, tied the horse to the rail by the bridle, ducked under the outside rails, and boarded a passing train for Calcutta. He sailed for home that night.

There's another story about one of J. C.'s great Cup horses, Shining Way, which is too good to pass over. This horse broke away from its groom coming back from the track and cantered off and out of sight. Passing the convent of the Little Sisters of the Poor, he spied the smooth green lawns and turned into the grounds to graze.

Now, the Little Sisters of the Poor had had a carriage horse which had taken them out daily to the offices of Calcutta's philanthropic business men. Eventually the old horse died. That night the nuns mentioned their loss respectfully in their prayers to the Lord. The following morning when they walked in the garden and saw the beautiful Shining Way grazing peacefully there, they knelt down and gave thanks for the gift. Then the groom harnessed Shining Way to the convent carriage and away went the Little Sisters to town.

In the meantime everybody in Calcutta except the nuns was searching for the missing Cup horse. A trainer who spied him pulling the modest equipage down the street couldn't believe his eyes. As soon as he had recovered his wits enough to report to J. C., the old man went shopping and bought the nuns a first-class carriage horse and a new carriage as well. The next day Shining Way won the Viceroy's Cup.

Bachelor's Wedding had won the Viceroy's Cup in 1914, but was beaten by the great Kiltoi the following year. In the Boxing Day meeting of 1916 the two horses were to oppose each other once more. This time, however, the owner of Bachelor's Wedding had a new contender running, Magyar, which stood second favourite to Kiltoi. The race was a mile and three-quarters, and poor Bachelor's Wedding started at 50-1. When the field got away, some of the outsiders set a hot pace. At the six-furlong post Magyar was running very smoothly and seemed to have Kiltoi's measure.

Bachelor's Wedding, with Py Ruiz riding, was way in the back in last place beside a horse belonging to the Maharaja of Cooch

Behar under a jockey named Paddy Firth. As the horses galloped along, Py Ruiz called out to Paddy that Bachelor's Wedding was in fine fettle and was rearing to go. Paddy said something about hoping Bachelor's Wedding would place, as a friend of his had drawn him in the Albert Club sweep. When Ruiz replied that he would not only place, he would win, Paddy laughed at him.

At the half-mile post, Ruiz started to give Bachelor's Wedding his head. I was standing near the rails under the winning-post when I saw that Magyar, which I had backed, had Kiltoi stone-cold at the distance post, and thought the race was over. The crowd thought so too, and began shouting, "Come *on*, Magyar !" as only a hundred thousand frenzied voices can shout. People started easing over to the betting ring to collect.

Suddenly down the middle of the track thundered a huge bay horse, his rider seeming to lift him at every stride. It was Bachelor's Wedding. Just in time, Ruiz caught up to Magyar and literally picked up his mount and hurled him over the finish line to win by half a head. I have seen hundreds of races since then, in Bombay, on the Continent, in England, and in America, but never have I seen a more exciting finish than that one.

The next year Kiltoi ran again, with Ruiz up, and won. But in the premier handicap of the cold-weather season, Ruiz had to concede about thirty pounds to a horse named One, and lost. One of the stewards said he hadn't pushed Kiltoi as he should have and mentioned that the whip had been used sparingly. Ruiz answered that he knew he was beaten by the weights and didn't want to knock Kiltoi about. The stewards told him to ride Kiltoi out, no matter what he thought.

Two weeks later the same horses met in another handicap. It was the most gruelling contest I have ever seen and enough to turn your stomach. At the four-furlong post Ruiz brought Kiltoi up beside One, still with the unfair difference in weights. Ruiz obeyed the stewards' orders. He brought the whip down at every stride like a farmer threshing wheat. He kept old Kiltoi neck and neck with One for those four long furlongs and got his head in front for the win.

In the paddock he dismounted. Poor Kiltoi stood there trembling, blood dripping from the whip and spur cuts in his side. Pointing to the horse, Ruiz told the stewards, "That horse will never face another starter". For two more years Kiltoi was entered in the big races. Every time he got to the starting-post he went haywire. He never ran again.

An old Belgian priest told me once with a smile that if racehorses were absolutely necessary for our happiness, we would find them in Heaven. I'm glad we didn't have to wait for that. It wasn't long before we had a still better course, and the second one became a boulevard, flanked with stores, houses, and even a jail. As the plant expanded, the course was moved again and only recently has given way to an airdrome.

Racing played a big part in making the initial seven-million-dollar Tata steel project into the gigantic industry it is today. With racing in their own backyard, so to speak, the boys stayed at home and made steel. And as the output of steel increased, wages rose and big bonuses became the order of the day. Men who had contracted to work for $250 a month began to draw bonuses of around $350 a month. Since the bonus was paid on the monthly output, the maximum could only be attained by every cog in the human machine doing his best. The men became their brothers' keepers. Heavy drinking ceased. And without any suggestions from the management.

In 1941, Tata's five furnaces produced a million and a quarter tons of pig-iron. For all we know, if there had been no racecourse in Jamshedpur back in those early days of the first World War, there might not be any Tata Steel Company today.

CHAPTER IV

TATA'S EXPANDS AND THE RUPEE CONTRACTS

BACK IN 1916, the roaring, pulsating, pounding, hissing organism that is a steel mill, and that in India was the booming Tata works, was, as it is now, running full out for war. And the war had brought its own set of special problems.

Warships and U-boats of the Central Powers lay in around the volcanic islands in the Straits of Messina and picked off at their convenience the Allied cargo-boats as fast as they came along. Nothing could get through. The English and the French desperately needed steel for use in the East and needed it, so to speak, on the spot. That meant Tata's. They vitally needed shells, and that meant Tata's, too. But we had no electric or special furnaces to make steel shells with.

Old Tut got that look in his eye that we all knew. He took a deep breath and went to work. We made steel shells on open-hearth furnaces, something like 8,000 tons of them. As far as I know, that was the only time that such a thing was ever done, and we did it well.

But then we had no way to press them. Old Tut arranged with every railway or shipbuilding workshop that had a lathe to *bore* out those five-inch rounds into shells. And, by God, it worked. Most of them went to Maude and Allenby in Mesopotamia, across the Persian Gulf by way of Karachi and Basra.

Still, on a twenty-four-hour schedule, Tata's couldn't keep up with the need for iron and steel. We were even turning out hames for the horses that pulled field guns. Our total output had reached 150,000 tons of steel a year. The company heads realized that in normal times, without war-time demands, India itself could absorb ten times that amount. We began to think about expanding.

The Tata company was still producing and selling rails on its contract with the Indian railways. It cost us seventy rupees a ton to make first-class rails which would pass the strict specifications. The contract price was 125 rupees. If a heat of steel was not good enough for rails, the heat was worked down until the carbon content was low enough for bars, rounds, etc. Then the bar-mills rolled the ingots into various products. But here was an anomaly. The high-test steel brought only 125 rupees from the railroads, while buyers waited at the door to take all the untested mill steel we could give them at prices ranging from 500 to 1,000 rupees a ton.

Then something happened which definitely set the directing minds of Tata's on a course of expansion. A shipment of ferro-manganese had gone to a Chicago firm at $37.50 a ton, f.o.b. Calcutta. This gave Tata's a nice profit. Between the time of dispatch from India and arrival in New York, that precious metal, indispensable in the making of commercial steel, had soared to around $300 a ton. The American firm sent Tata's another cheque for $75,000. They had made an additional profit and wished Tata's to have half of it. They offered to buy another 10,000 tons at the market price. Tata's could not accept the order. The plant had only two blast furnaces then, needed for Tata's own steel. To make ferro-manganese, Tata would have to build another furnace.

Jamshedjee Tata urged Charles Page Perin to come out to India with proposals for increasing the plant's output. Normally, a progressive company would add a blast furnace, a couple of open-hearth furnaces, a few mills to diversify the output, and perhaps revamp existing equipment. When Perin arrived in Bombay he had some plans along these lines which would have meant increasing the capital of the company from about seven to a possible fourteen million dollars. He advised caution. Besides the new furnaces, he would add an extra driving engine, a small plate-mill, and another bar-mill. Altogether, production would rise from 150,000 to 225,000 tons a year. Perin's view was that of any good engineer: build slowly and solidly and conserve your resources.

At the directors' meetings at Jamshedpur, many tentative ideas were advanced for stepping up production to meet the growing Indian market. One evening after dinner, Perin produced his modest outline, asked the directors for their undivided attention, and spoke for fifteen minutes, technically and conservatively. World markets were abnormal because of the war, he said, but the normal demand would increase considerably in India, so that Tata's could feel perfectly safe in expanding tenfold over a period of years, without being forced to export into a competitive foreign market.

Dorabjee Tata had a quite different and more dynamic plan for the company's part in the new India. He recalled to the quiet semicircle of men, intent on his words, the dream that had inspired the founding of the company, Jamshedjee's vision of a self-supporting, strong, industrial India, of ships built in India carrying goods made in India to far-flung markets across the seas. Now that Perin had proved that he could transmute Indian iron into steel of high quality with Indian labour, Tata proposed first a vote of absolute confidence in the engineer. Then, turning to Perin, he said gravely that whatever he needed to expand the plant so as eventually to supply India's total steel requirements was his to command. And, Tata concluded, all new capital would come from Indian investors.

There was a moment of silence as the men around the table realized the sweeping significance of the pledge. Then Charles Page Perin rolled up his unpretentious proposals. And with them he discarded the conservative Perin. Men of later generations who have never seen the grand old man, usually refer to him as "that extravagant Mr. Perin". But he was neither to blame for the prodigal spending that followed nor should he receive all the credit for its benefits. It was typical Tata courage and Tata initiative that now launched the company on its vast new programme. Perin bought plant and equipment at war prices. After the war he could have got the lot for half what they cost. But after the war there would not have been any new plant, and the old one would have shut down under the flood of cheap steel which glutted the unprotected world markets. Dorabjee Tata was everywhere, hurrying the work, prodding the local management. He predicted a serious depression after the war, like that which followed the Civil War. The new plant must be ready to run full out when the depression had passed.

The man who worked most closely with Perin, however, was the former economics professor, B. P. Padshah, who still refused to take from the company more than just enough to cover his frugal living, his books, and his travelling expenses. Padshah would not wear shoes made of cowhide. He refused to ride in a horse-drawn vehicle because, he said, the animal had no way of telling him whether or not it was pleased to perform the service for him. Some years ago, at a meeting of a scholarly London club, seven men were named who really understood Einstein's theory of relativity, men who used calculus much as ordinary people use subtraction and addition. Padshah was one of the seven.

He used to drive Perin wild at first because he had his own way of going about things. In the middle of a serious technical discussion Padshah would go off into a description of the future India, with its giant fleet of merchant ships, manned by Indian sailors. Or he would open his desk drawer, take out a book of poetry and read from it. Perin would despair of ever accomplishing anything.

I remember once in 1922 when we were in the middle of a strike and Padshah was doing his best to settle it amicably, working long and hard hours. But he had to have his relaxation. I dragged myself home one evening to find half a dozen women I knew there, listening to Padshah reading aloud from Browning's *Ivan Ivanovitch.* He asked me if I liked Browning's poetry. I said no. Then I remembered something Chauncey Brewster Tinker had said once at Yale, and quoted him—without credit. I preferred Tennyson to Browning, I said, because Tennyson's poetry was like gentle waves stealing in on white sands, bringing peace and quiet, while Browning always made me think of billows smashing against a rock-bound coast. Padshah was delighted, and afterwards told everybody that I was one of the few steel men who really understood the beauty of poetry. I didn't disillusion him.

Both Perin and Padshah were enthusiasts, and when enthusiasts met together nothing is impossible. A small point is discussed early in the morning, it is discarded for something entirely different over the luncheon table, built up during the afternoon, dreamed about that night, and made a reality the next day. The starting point of the new project was the blooming-mill, through which all the steel for the other mills would have to miss.

The blooming-mill then in use was an adequate affair, driven by the same steam engine that ran the rail and structural mill. Ingots were brought from the open-hearth soaking pits and put into the blooming-mill. The resulting blooms were charged to a reheating furnace. Whenever the furnace was filled with blooms and they had reached the right temperature, one simply declutched the engine from the bloomer, then attached it to the rail mills. Simultaneous operation of both mills was impossible. Perin's first step was to instal a separate engine for the bloomer, and production rose immediately.

Now, electrically driven blooming-mills were in common use in the United States long before 1917, and the old steam-driven mill became a nightmare to Perin. It was obvious to him that Tata's needed a new, electric bloomer, one large enough to take care of all production increases for years to come. Complete with soaking pits and buildings, such a blooming-mill would cost from three to five million dollars, and would accomplish only a slight boost in production. Perin didn't see how could swing it. He sat around with Padshah for days mulling over figures.

They came to the matter of imported galvanized-iron sheets, which India had been bringing in some 300,000 tons a year for a long time. There were also the 50,000 and more tons of tin plate used every year by the Burma Oil Company to make kerosene and petrol cans. While Padshah and Perin were trying to justify spending the money for the new bloomer, the Burma Oil Company came along with the answer. They offered to go into partnership with Tata's in a tin-plate company, furnish two-thirds of the capital, and take up the debentures, if Tata's would make them sheet bar. Here was an outlet for another 100,000 tons of ingots a year. Tata was to start manufacturing immediately. Tin bar could be rolled on the same mills as sheet bar. India was still importing over 100,000 tons of merchant bars yearly, flats and rounds. But billets to feed a large merchant mill could be rolled on a new sheet-bar and billet mill. The market was there, suddenly, before their eyes. All they needed were the new mills.

Raising production to half a million tons of ingots a year meant more blast furnaces to furnish the pig-iron requirements; then new coke-ovens to supply fuel for the blast furnaces. To ensure a steady flow of fuel, they would have to buy or lease more collieries. Nor was that the end. They must locate new iron-ore properties, manganese-ore veins, limestone quarries. The new steel venture took on exact shape, even though its proportions were still staggering to both Padshah and Perin. Sir Dorab and his brother, Sir Ratan Tata, and their cousin, R. D. Tata, as well as the board of directors, were backing them, however, and when Perin estimated a capital increase of seven to thirty million dollars, a new prospectus was immediately issued for subscriptions. The Maharaja of Gwalior came forward with an offer for the whole $21,000,000 worth of second preference, 7 per cent, accumulative shares. New deferred shares with a par value of thirty rupees were snapped up the day they appeared on the Bombay exchange at a premium of 370 rupees per share. And new common shares were absorbed within a few days.

The war boom was on. Soon the Peninsular Locomotive Company, the Jute Mill Foundries, Agricultural Implements, Ltd., Hume Pipe Company, Indian Wire Products, Indian Enamelware Company, all to be situated in Jamshedpur, placed their shares on the market. They ran advertisements in the Calcutta and Bombay papers, as required by law, most of them printing across the announcements, "This advertisement is published in order to comply with the Companies Act. Please note that all shares have been subscribed."

The dynamic Perin, happiest when he was working under high pressure, returned to New York, enlarged his offices, and put three hundred engineers and draughtsmen to work. He took two new partners, Steward M. Marshall, a fine engineer who was satisfied with no project until it worked out to a decimal point and two noughts, and energetic Frank L. Estep, who thought that God put mountains on earth simply for men to tear into them and push them about.

I found out just how energetic he was a few years ago. Estep was in Moscow doing a job for the Soviet Government. I was on my way to the Ruhr district in Germany and met him in Düsseldorf. After a quick lunch he dragged me off to Duisberg to visit a steel plant in Boakum. The next day we arrived early in the morning at the Hamborn plant, then, next to Gary, Indiana, the largest in the world. Getting back to the hotel in Düsseldorf about eight at night, we discussed drawings, figures, and data, with Estep making rough sketches of various ideas which had occurred to him during the day. We worked until three, and he woke me up at six-thirty to catch the train for Hantrop, where there were a couple of blast furnaces that were breaking records. The German company operating them claimed they were producing iron on the world's lowest coke consumption from iron ore. Once there we knew the truth. They were charging only half ore, the other half was scrap iron and steel. I have found a good many German industrial miracles equally exaggerated.

When, after some days of this sort of routine, we arrived at the Thyssen works in the Ruhr Valley, Estep was as fresh as when he started. He was the most tireless man I ever knew.

Actual wonders were being performed in America during the early period of Tata expansion by a newly developed method of producing steel, a combination of the Bessemer converter and the open-hearth processes now called the duplex process. Plants on the Lackawanna Steel Company at Buffalo and at South Chicago had got such results that another plant had been installed at Gary. As a matter of fact, whenever the scrap market rises and there is a strong demand for soft steel, it pays to use the duplex process. By the straight open-hearth procedure, one charges scrap and molten pig-iron and usually taps at 125-ton heat in something over ten hours. By the duplex process one charges raw, highly oxidized steel from a Bessemer converter and generally taps 125 tons of mild steel in two hours. Using the duplex in India, we have tapped as much as 1,400 tons of low carbon steel in twenty-four hours from one furnace.

Perin at once saw that the set-up in India was ideal for the duplex method, since scrap was not plentiful and pig-iron was cheap. He informed Tata's that his new ingot-producing plant would give them 30, 000 tons a month with two furnaces and that the buildings for a third furnace would be laid out at the same time to be ready when needed. He started with a 600-ton mixer storage for hot metal from the blast furnaces, then increased the size and capacity of that mixer to 1300 tons within a month. Those figures were startling then; today, with the third furnace running, Tata's produces upwards of 65,000 tons a month.

Perin's plans naturally caused some excitement in Jamshedpur and a flurry of trans-Pacific cables.

Padshah to Perin: "Where are you going to get the molten pig-iron for your new process?"

The answer: "I am designing two new 500-ton blast furnaces."

Padshah cabled: "Where are you going to get the coke for the new blast furnaces?"

Perin replied : "I am calling for tenders for three new batteries of by-product coke ovens."

"Where do you expect to get suitable coking coal?"

"Please buy the Jamadoba colliery. I am coming out to secure leases on other high-grade coke bodies."

So that, some 12,000 miles apart, the two men settled in a few days questions that might have consumed weeks of discussion. Perin's office force was thrown into high gear. Between 1917 and 1920 his firm designed and sent out 700,000 tracings and over 3,000,000 blue-prints. A new blooming-mill, guaranteed for 900,000 tons of ingots a year, a 300,000-ton rail and structural mill, a 500,000-ton sheet-bar and billet-mill, a 100,000-ton merchant-mill, and a 50,000-ton sheet-mill—all these took shape on paper in New York and not long after began to break the skyline in Jamshedpur. Nor was this all. A $2,000,000 boiler-plant equipped with automatic stokers for firing coal was ordered and dispatched and twenty-four gas-fired boilers at $1,000,000. The General Electric Company furnished several million dollars' worth of both large and small turbines.

Perin accomplished these gigantic projects under the most difficult conditions. For America was now in the war, and every plant in the country was working overtime turning out war supplies. The shipbuilding programme had sent the price of steel plates to incredible figures, and Perin's new duplex-furnace building alone called for 37,000 tons of fabricated steel, which was cut to order and drilled ready for erection. When Perin added a large 96-inch plate-mill and its housing structures, just the buildings for the new plant totalled 115,000 tons of fabricated steel. These were bought at war prices and shipped to India.

When the Armistice came, Americans knew of it early in the morning of November 11, 1918, but we, on the other side of the world,, were just coming home from work when we heard, and only received confirmation shortly after daybreak on November

12. When old Tutwiler learned that the war was over he declared the following day a holiday at the mills. No furnace was to be charged up after midnight, and the morning-shift crews could go home as soon as their heats had been tapped. It was the first holiday many of those sturdy Britishers and Americans had had since 1916. Besides their bonuses, they had been drawing thirty-two and thirty-three days' pay per month because of double pay for Sunday during the whole two years. They needed their holiday—and at that rate they could afford to pay for one.

During the war the local bar had been put on short hours, from one-thirty until three p.m. and from five until eight in the evening. We called the place the Blood Tub. Old Tut gave orders that the Blood Tub was to stay open from noon until nine at night. I was there early and so was nearly everybody else in town. Two brothers, Britishers, named Jim and Tom, were holding down one end of the bar. Tom had been invalided home suffering from shell shock after three years' service and had come to take up his former trade of steel-making in India. He looked fairly serene this day in the Blood Tub, but I had seen him morose many a time, with some awful, nameless fear clouding his mind. It wasn't long after our Armistice celebration, I remember, that I congratulated Tom on a fine job of repairing the bottom and banks of a big H.O. furnace. Despite his pleasure at being praised, there was a withdrawn, fearful look in Tom's eyes when he turned to me. "I'll never do a better job than that," he said. He never did; in fact, that was his last job. After work that Saturday, he went to his bungalow, shaved, and powdered his face. He picked up a double-barrelled shotgun, sat down in a chair, leaned his chin on the muzzle, and blew the top of his head off.

Standing next to Tom in the Blood Tub on November 12 was Big Fellow, from Tennessee. Big Fellow hadn't tasted a drop since 1916. He always said he'd drunk his share. But now he felt he had a right to celebrate. Just three drinks and he'd stop. He ordered three double whiskys, and told the bearer to bring three double gins for a chaser.

Old Tut had said, "Let the boys get together and have a bit of a sing-song". And, besides the shouted greetings and relieved, hilarious laughter, there was plenty of sing-song. The boys sang until the walls shook with the roar of their voices. The Britishers stood up and gave us *God Save the King*. The Americans knew the tune and sang it, too, some of them using the words of *America*. Then the Yanks sounded off in *The Star-Spangled Banner,* and the boys from the Tees-side joined in two or three choruses of *Dixie*. I thought they'd burst their brawny, corded throats.

Then, almost as though at a signal, the volume of sound diminished, faltered, and ceased altogether. There was no rejoicing now in the flushed faces. In a heavy silence, the men stood quietly, looking into their half-empty glasses, their thoughts far away in other times and places, with other people. They were remembering their dead.

Old Jock walked in. A more dour man never breathed, nor a better man on an open-hearth furnace. He had lost two sons, and his third was crippled for life. Jock caught the mood of the place and his eyes blurred. In a low voice he said to me, "May God bless us and keep us out of another war !" Jay, from Carlyle, pushed through the crowd, silent as always, and ordered a double Scotch with a Bass chaser, or what we called a puddler and a helper. I knew his thoughts were with the brothers and the son who would never come back. It was a homely scene, the smoky, dimly lighted room, peopled with silent mourners, fellows of little guile, fine steel-workers and fine men.

Shortly before the Armistice, Dorabjee Tata had warned the shareholders at a meeting that prices would change radically when hostilities ceased, that they could not expect to go on receiving unheard-of dividends. Tata's deferred shares had paid over 200 per cent for the year, and he begged the investors to be careful and the gamblers to be wary. As a result of that speech, Tata Deferred dropped from 1900 to around 1300, and Common from 320 to 260 in a mad scramble.

But no one really believed Sir Dorab, at least none of the gamblers did, and the shares rose again, Tata's as usual leading the rest of the market. That whole period through 1918 and 1919 was characterized by the wildest enthusiasm and thirst for expansion. Indian printers worked night and day getting out prospectuses for the new companies. Home Rule for India was never mentioned. The minds of India's politicians and business men had been engrossed with the war, and the winning of it. Now the British in India hoped that the question of freedom had been forgotten, or that at least the politicians could keep peace for a while.

The local British bureaucrats knew well the tenets of the diehard Lord Roberts, whose memoirs of his forty-one years in India were published, ironically, with such success during the year of Queen Victoria's Jubilee. In the book Roberts says that ninety-nine out of every hundred Indians are "absolutely devoice of any idea of civil responsibilities", and that we (the British "have not only the determination, but also the ability, to maintain our supremacy in India against all assailants". Few of the British in India, however, had heard of a quiet little man, a lawyer who had done yeoman's service for the Empire during the Boer War, a man who had read

Roberts' book years before and determined that some day the world must be shown how wrong its doctrines were. His name was Mohandas K. Gandhi.

India had sent 750,000 well-trained soldiers and 500,000 labourers overseas to Palestine, Egypt, Mesopotamia, and to France. Many an Indian Sipahi had died in Flanders and, in death beside his British officers and fellow soldiers from the far-flung Empire, had forever disproved the mouldy adage that one Tommy was equal to ten Indian soldiers. The lucky ones who lived disproved it, too, with their heroism. So that when the survivors came home, they were filled with a feeling of equality new to them, a feeling which was to spread out from them in widening circles and to have its own effect on the temper of the people.

King George V, keenly aware of the staggering debt India had piled on her people for the prosecution of the war, sent Edwin Samuel Montagu, Secretary of State for India, to survey the situation with the Viceroy, Lord Chelmsford. As soon as they should receive the joint report of these two men, the King's Ministers were to take immediate action on the Home Rule dispute. British business men in India were pleased. Surely the Indians would behave now for a few years. The resulting 1919 boom in shares on the Calcutta and Bombay exchanges made America's bull market look like a schoolboy prank.

One old Parsi, who had never made more than fifty dollars a month in his life, came to be called King of Tata's Deferred because he rode the shares up to the top, then turned bear and slid down the hill with them. He saved enough out of his killing to buy an iron-clad annuity for a quarter of a million dollars, and gambled in earnest with the surplus. With his host of followers, that old boy rocked the market. It was his ambition to own a mansion on Malabar Hill, and to do that he would have to be worth at least a *crore* of rupees, or three and a third million dollars. Six months later he was broke, except, of course, for that annuity.

Most Indian companies call up only 10 per cent of the subscribed capital on issue, the remainder is called up when needed. Once the shares are listed on the exchange they are anybody's gambling medium. Like the Tata shares. When they were offered, a number of us bought a few for seven and a half rupees a share. We received our scrip and put it aside. When they rose to seven and a half plus a premium of fifteen, I wrote to my bank to sell. They asked for the scrip. While we were writing back and forth, the shares had gone to twenty rupees premium. I decided to ride for a while. Two months later I sold for forty rupees premium. I had made 750 per cent on my investment.

Not everybody was so lucky, or in the same way. The Irishman, V. G. Piggott, was my racing partner at the time. He had discovered some phosphate deposits and formed a company to quarry the rock. Ten rupees were called up on the 100-rupee par value shares. Within a few months those shares were selling at sixty rupees premium, in spite of the fact that the company had not yet even bought any machinery. They had nothing but a few holes in the ground and the geologists' estimate. There was a ready-made market for the phosphate, however, in the enormous Indian tea-gardens.

Just when the phosphate boom was the talk of Clive Street, it was discovered that another company held leases on the property with the right to mine minerals. Of course, they couldn't mine phosphate rock, since under the wording of the act it was not an ore or a mineral, but a rock. But that rock contained a fair amount of iron. Therefore it was claimed that the phosphate company was removing iron ore with a high phosphorus content. The shares took a slight tumble and the little fellows got out.

Then it was realized that while the tea-gardens could use calcium phosphate in its soluble form, the company's phosphates were the insoluble kind, which is fine for raising the phosphorus content in pig-iron for the basic Bessemer process, but worthless for the open-hearth process. Like hundreds of other infant companies floated at this time, this one never outgrew its swaddling clothes.

The price of silver followed the rising market graph and the silver rupee went up in proportion. Normally worth one shilling and fourpence, or roughly thirty-two cents, in the autumn of 1919 the rupee was worth two shillings and eightpence. So that, while India could buy on foreign markets at an enormous advantage, she could not sell abroad on the competitive world markets. When I left India on home leave in the spring of 1920, I could buy a dollar for 2.35 rupees. In September a dollar cost me 4.5 rupees. My pay was practically halved. Whereas the rupee had been more or less pegged to the gold sovereign at fifteen before the war, the Old Lady of Threadneedle Street now pegged it at ten, thus making India a fine market for British goods, but keeping Indian capital goods at home.

Had that rate of exchange been maintained for long, Indian industries would have disappeared, no matter how cheaply she could buy goods and equipment from England. For instance, Great Britain makes a ton of tested structural steel and lands it in a Calcutta warehouse for an all-in cost, including profit, of ten pounds, or 150 rupees, a ton. Tata's makes a ton of structural steel and lands it in Calcutta by rail for 120 rupees a ton. Tata's can compete with England at a fair profit if they sell their steel for 150 rupees—and England makes a little more or a little less.

With the rupee gold ratio at 10 to 1, England can, if she wants to be ruthless, sell her steel for 120 rupees a ton, which is what it costs Tata's to produce it, and soon drive her Indian competitor into bankruptcy.

On the other hand, let us say that London markets are stable and India ships manganese ore to England. She receives her fair gold price for it, but when she sends the proceeds out home to pay her miners and the taxes she loses 33⅓ per cent compared to the normal exchange. Or perhaps a British syndicate owns the manganese mines. That syndicate can export the ore to England and sell it, turn the money into tested steel beams, export those British beams to Calcutta and undersell Tata on the Indian market. When the local competition has been wiped out, the syndicate can raise the price to whatever level it pleases.

India was heavily in debt to England after the war. Indians were told that the new rate of exchange would decrease the debt. All they had to do was to sell their capital goods and repay the amount owing. But with keen British competition and with Belgium and Germany dumping capital goods on the world markets at rock bottom, how and where could India sell her goods?

Most of the Americans working in India liked the prevailing rate of exchange, since they could ship their rupees home and buy dollars more cheaply, but there was one American there who suffered from it. He was an engineer who had offered his services to Tata's for $1,000 a month, payable in dollars. Tata's earmarked $24,000, bought some time before, to cover two years' salary. When the man arrived in Jamshedpur and found that his three general foremen were getting around 2,700 rupees a month, or much more than he did, he blew up and charged the company with deliberately cheating him. That man would never drink a whisky and soda; he said it was too damned un-American. So now he took to dry Martinis. In less than a year we sent him home to save his life.

That man and his dry Martinis was one of the few lighter touches in an otherwise grim situation, in which the plight of the cotton-mill owners and workers was perhaps the darkest general factor, for cotton was still the life of India. The English Lancashire mills were working three shifts, sending cotton to Indian wharves and warehouses, where it flooded out the local product and found ready customers. Mills in Bombay had to shut down. Those mills which did manage to hang on took huge losses, cut wages, and in a frantic effort to survive, threw in funds which for years had been built up into depreciation accounts.

What for the rest of the world was a comparatively mild depression brought India to the brink of an abyss. The rising ferment of apprehension and uncertainty in the minds of the millions of India's workers made a fertile bedding ground for ideas seeping into the country from Russia, ideas intended to fertilize the fallow collective will of the worker to his own protection.

If the cotton industry was in dire straits, the young steel industry was in peril of its life. No one had worried about paying for the mushroom expansion of Tata's during the period of 1917-1920 when the company was piling up huge profits. The new capitalization could not be expected to provide the needed amount, not at war levels, nor actually to do more than pay for barely half the cost. But any equipment bought then at any price yielded returns, and it was felt the money would surely come from somewhere. But the company had figured on 310 rupees buying $100. And in 1919 it took 240 rupees; by 1921, when the big payments began to come due, it sometimes took 450 rupees to purchase $100. The Tatas had to go to the London markets to float a loan, to plead for £2,000,000 sterling at 8 per cent.

Then, just as Dorabjee Tata had foreseen, India was flooded with cheap Continental steel smelted out of scrap from the French and Flemish battlefields, sometimes selling below its works cost. Since the selling price of all steel except rails was dependent on prices of Continental steel, profits vanished. By the time the duplex furnaces and new mills were ready for operation it looked very much as though the company was not going to weather the depression of 1921 and 1922. Old Blaser, our Swiss engineer, had invested his savings in Tata second preference shares at par and they had skidded to the bottom. In his usual pithy way he remarked, 'If we lose ten rupees every time we sell a ton of pig-iron or steel, how many rupees will we lose when we sell half a million tons from the new plant?"

Not only were boatloads of Belgian steel raffled off and dumped in Calcutta and Bombay for next to nothing, but Tata's urgently needed enormous sums of money for erecting blacksmith and pattern shops, foundries, new machine-shops, and for the maintenance of machinery to go in them. Then money had to be found for the fifty miles of railroad added to the original seventeen miles inside the parent plant. Eighteen new locomotives and some 400 freight cars joined the company's rolling stock. Only the optimism of a few men kept the company alive in 1922.

The outlook was so dark that at one memorable meeting of the company's directors one of the men suggested that the company go to the Government and ask to be taken over. Immediately R. D. Tata, father of the present chairman of the board, angrily jumped to his feet and, pounding on the table for emphasis, shouted that that day would never come as long as he lived. But he had more than indignation back of his determination. He had a concrete proposal.

The machinery of negotiation was set in motion and the Government shown that no steel company could survive the existing unfair competition from tariff-free Continental steel. R. D. Tata and T. W. Tutwiler went to Delhi with figures to prove that if it were not for the cost of the extensions, the company would be in the clear. The Government granted a sizable loan on condition that Tutwiler had complete charge.

A Tariff Board was set up to study the situation. It framed a protective Act which, when passed by the Legislature, saved the company from sure ruin. Nowadays, under peacetime conditions no protective tariff is necessary. The infant industry has grown up under the wing of a far-sighted Government. For the past five years Tata's has paid its shareholders higher returns than any other steel company in the world, partly because of the Tatas, Perin, and men like Tutwiler, and largely because of the staying hand of a much-maligned Government.

CHAPTER V

LABOUR PAINS

WHEN I WENT on home leave from India early in 1920, I didn't stay very long in America. For one thing, I was anxious to take my brand new American wife back with me, to explore with her as much as possible of the East on the long way round, by way of Japan and China.

For another, I found myself a foreigner in America. Occasionally the strains of *Dardenella*, or *Swanee River*, or a bit of *Chu Chin Chow* on a phonograph or in a restaurant would make me feel at home. But I began counting the days that must pass before I could set out once more for the East.

We enjoyed the trip like a couple of Cook's tourists. Shipping schedules were still disrupted from the war, and we had plenty of time between boats to have a look-see at every port. Between Shanghai and Hongkong cholera broke out among the crew of the old tub that had been the best we could get. We were afraid we would be quarantined in Hongkong. Fortunately, a dear old fellow-passenger, a former Governor of Arizona who was on his way to Siam as American Minister, took us ashore with him in an official launch. The ex-Governor asked my advice about warding off any lurking cholera germs. I prescribed a steady diet of Napoleon brandy, one with every meal, two between meals, and a double helping on going to bed. He seemed to enjoy the treatment. And apparently it worked.

In September we arrived in India. During my brief absence of eight months India had changed. I hardly recognized Jamshedpur. A whole new subdivision enlarged the town. New and larger bungalows were everywhere. I was assigned to quarters in another part of the town. The former site of my stable now held the rather palatial home of an American missionary. Off to the left was a new club house and half a dozen tennis-courts, besides some sixty capacious tents housing part of the new crowd of engineers who were working on the expansion of the plant. Out on the hill called Burma Mines more houses and tents sheltered the American structural-iron workers.

There were other changes. Industrial India had been inundated with Russian pamphlets. The workmen no longer sat around the sand-beds at night telling stories of the great past. They held their heads high and looked you in the eye. They talked of Home Rule and of a new Government. There had been a wave of strikes all over the industrial sections. Tata's workmen had walked out without notice the preceding February and had stayed out for a month. Their grievances had been examined and they received, among other things, a 25 per cent wage increase.

I immediately noticed a disturbing difference in the attitude of some of the men towards each other. The new American engineers, many of whom were only a few years out of college, didn't mix with the American and British steel operators. The old-timers went to the Institute, danced the waltz, two-step, and even the Lancers, the newcomers danced the fox-trot, the Lame Duck, and the tango at the club. They disdained our whiskies-and-sodas, insisting on cocktails and other poisonous 7° concoctions. The old crowd talked of horses and men; the youngsters of golf, dancing, and women; they seemed to regard their stay in India as part of a world pleasure tour. These Johnny-come-latelys turned up their noses at our table-stake poker in favour of bridge, at which they thought they were pretty good—until they bucked some of the Englishmen.

The structural-iron workers who came out to put up the new plant, however, were familiar types. Like most men in their trade, they were hard-hitting fellows who worked well and spent their time from Saturday noon to Sunday midnight at table-stake poker. They would fight at the slightest provocation, but seldom started a row. Twenty months after those boys got to Jamshedpur, the last rivets were driven into the new buildings.

Two of the structural-iron fellows, Bill and George, who batched together, left India with fat bank accounts. Every week-end they ran a stud-poker game at their diggings. On Saturday after work they stopped at the Blood Tub and let the boys there know the game was about to begin. They bought six or eight dozen bottles of beer, a case of Scotch, and about 200 lbs. of ice, loaded it into their flivver, and were off. This was the way the game was run: all drinks were free to the players—that is, no man had to dig down into his jeans for the price—but Bill and George "raked" all pots in the game up to one rupee, or thirty-seven cents, until the drinks were paid for. Sometimes they went right on raking the pots late into the night—for "future" drinks. Since the hosts supplied the boys with food as well, nobody cared how many pots they raked. Still, more than once I have seen them pay out 100 rupees for the liquor and sandwiches and pay themselves back more than 500 rupees.

Bill and George certainly cleaned the country boys. To my personal knowledge neither of them ever played a game of poker unless he was cold sober. But they were both good actors. Early in the game one of them or both would appear to have drunk too much. Bill sometimes held up the play, saying he couldn't see the cards. George always told him he must have had too many at the Blood Tub and to go to bed. Bill never did, and neither man ever lost. They played airtight stud, waiting until they held a big pair, then playing the cards to the limit. Their motto was: "With aces or kings, back to back, never let an opponent draw a fourth card". Since the game was always for table stakes, few players risked drawing a fourth.

George and Bill would toss a coin for $500, but they wouldn't risk five dollars on a horse race. When anybody passed the hat to collect for a widow, they tossed in 100-rupee notes. Neither of them ever spent a cent of their salaries; furthermore, they saved a lot of their poker winnings. Bill once told me that the man who said a sucker was born every minute didn't know what he was talking about. "Confidentially," Bill said, "they come every minute, but in litters."

At the plant and in the town a great number of Indians, I noticed, now wore little muslin caps. I talked to a fine strapping fellow about it, a college graduate who worked for me on the blast furnaces. "It is Gandhi's idea," he said, "a sign of the times, the beginning of an India-for-Indians movement. Somehow a peaceful solution will be reached," he continued. "If not for us, then for our children, and if not for them, then for their children. Some day we will be free."

Not long after our arrival cholera hit the town from an influx of a Central Province tribe, the Chattisgarhis, who came looking for jobs. Our pest-house overflowed with cholera-stricken Indians.

Cholera is as a rule not only fatal to the patient but to the attending nurse, and we had a shortage of nurses. My college graduate asked leave for the duration of the plague. I thought he had the wind up. Instead, he wanted to help out in the pest-house. As soon as the plague should be over, he would return to work.

Of all the changes I could perceive, the deepest was apparent not so much in the relations of some of the new men to the old-timers, but in the attitude of the workmen in general towards the management. The old friendly spirit of affection which our labourer had felt for his foreman had been replaced by an acute distrust not far from hate. The workman was not insolent, but his manner was. This unhappy state of things, the exact antithesis of all that the Tatas had wanted for their plant, came about as a result of the strike. When it began, the men were not truculent; they seemed to be enjoying a well-earned holiday, and spent the days laughing and telling stories.

Then a few of them conceived it to be a great joke on the company if they should tear up the rails connecting the works and the railway station, thus cutting off raw materials and coal supplies. The commanding officers of the troops which the Government had sent to the area to maintain order were promptly informed of the mischief afoot.

Soldiers detailed to prevent the men from destroying plant equipment ordered the prankish strikers to leave. They emphatically refused. The soldiers were ordered to load and take aim. The men, like overgrown children, laughed at the soldiers and their officer. The order was then given to fire. Thirteen strikers were killed and many more taken to the hospital. It has always made me feel a little better to remember that no Government official gave that fateful order.

Although the strike was ended not long after, the men did not forget the death of their fellows. They turned from quiet, conscientious workers to aggressive men who did just what they were paid for and not a bit more. For several years, on the anniversary of that day, the Indians observed one hour's silence.

The men who had led the strikers now became their official leaders. They formed a union which many of the Tata workers joined. Meanwhile there were strikes in other parts of India. The men said, "Strike first, formulate demands later". It became the custom to call in political leaders to plead the cause of labour. Labour leaders became political-minded.

I have never heard of a union in America or in England declaring a strike against a management that had its back to the wall. But in spite of the 25 per cent wage increase granted the labourers at Tata's in 1920 when the company was paying dividends, in 1922, when the company's earnings barely covered depreciation and the interest on debentures, the workmen struck again, for another raise.

The brooding tension culminated simply and unexpectedly one day when we were rushing one of our new blast furnaces, hoping to light her up early in September. An American engineer was urging on a crowd of Indian pipe-fitters. One of them, a Mohammedan, stopped work to say his prayers, kneeling with palms outstretched, bowing to Allah. The American was a university graduate who had been in India for two years and should have known better. He not only reprimanded the man, but kicked him. News of the grave insult to a Mohammedan spread instantly through the plant from man to man. Twenty thousand workers laid down their tools.

This time we tried to operate one blast furnace and two or three steel furnaces. For the first two weeks we found it almost impossible to operate even one furnace, although we had plenty of Europeans to run it and hundreds of Indians who were ready to work. Indian labour had learned the art of sabotage. While the men were busy, someone would climb aloft and shut off the water-feed pipes, only to sneak up and turn them on again after bronze plates or tuyere coolers had burned or cracked. Two or three times the furnace got an awful drenching before the leak was discovered. After we had fought that old furnace for ten days, we put European guards around it and got perfect operation.

During this strike, outside labour leaders came to town, some of whom realized that the men had chosen a bad time for their demonstration. They were stoned for saying so. Not until the men were reminded of the precarious financial position of Tata's, making any further wage raise unlikely, did they see that they had made a mistake. The strike was settled eventually, and by the same American engineer who started it, but quite without his volition, or even his knowledge.

When the walk-out has lasted some three weeks, the American, walking home from a round of golf with his house-mate, dropped into the bungalow opposite mine for a short one and a rubber of bridge. The two men found the friend they sought trying to put together a gun he had borrowed for a week-end shoot. The engineer's room-mate took over the assembling of the gun and sat down on a bench in front of the fireplace, while his pal started playing the piano. The golfer who was fixing the gun slipped it together expertly and was about to pass it to his host when his finger accidentally touched the trigger and he sent a bullet through the heart of the man at the piano. The engineer lived just long enough to whisper, "You've killed me".

I rushed across the street as soon as I heard the shot, but the man was already dead. We dressed the body in clean linen and a fresh suit. A coffin was brought around by midnight. By two in the morning it was necessary to shut and seal the coffin, since in the tropics decay sets in very rapidly. We buried him just after sunrise.

In a matter of minutes the tidings of this man's death had spread through the town on the wings of the wind. The devout Mohammedans looked upon it as an act of God. Their fellow workman had been avenged. Two days later the entire staff returned to work unconditionally. And although the company refused to recognize their union for three years, they worked hard and well.

The death of thirteen Indians had ended the first strike. The death by accident of one American ended the second.

Indians were not alone in absorbing the strike virus during the early days of labour's struggle for freedom under the banner of Mahatma Gandhi. Nearly all the European workmen at the Tin Plate Company, a Tata subsidiary, were men from South Wales. They had signed contracts to work in India for a stipulated salary, with bonuses on production at a base rate to be set after the new mills had had a fair run. When the first two of the nine mills had been in operation for a short while, the management compared their production with that of the American and Welsh mills, and even allowing for local climatic conditions, they made a very poor showing. A child could see that the rollers were holding back, hoping that the management would set a low base rate.

Frank Estep happened to be in India at the time. The general manager and the superintendent of the Tin Plate Company had come up from the ranks and knew their stuff. The three men decided to take the Welsh boys on. They took over one mill, worked it for an eight-hour period, and turned out a remarkably big tonnage. Then they bet the three best Welsh boys that they could beat them the following day. That was an exciting race. Naturally the Welsh rollers won the bet, but by only a few boxes of tin plate. The losers paid for plenty of drinks all round. Then the management announced the base rate, figured on the production of the Welsh rollers.

The contract workers decided to strike. They walked out confidently. After a few weeks their committee called on the Deputy Commissioner some forty miles away in the old town of Chaibasa. They stated their case in a long and courteous hearing. The Commissioner, Jim Scott, then excused himself, leaving a supply of cold beer and a decanter of whisky for the men, and drove to Jamshedpur to hear the company's side of the case. He also read the contracts, signed and stamped in London and again in India. Back in Chaibasa, he told the committee the men didn't have a leg to stand on, they had broken their contracts and forfeited their return passage to England. He advised them to go to Jamshedpur and throw themselves on the mercy of the company.

The committee were pretty well oiled by this time, and they couldn't believe their ears. Back they went, however, meek as could be, and did what they were told. The next day the strike was over. The men accepted the base rate and turned out production equal to the American mills and higher than their countrymen were making on similar mills in South Wales. They later admitted that they hadn't tried before. But even without their admission, nobody could have suspected Scott of being partial. He was one of the finest types of Britishers, although you had to know him to realize the man was not a snob. He had a manner as cold as snow on a convent roof.

To go back a couple of years. Tata's and its subsidiaries were not the only companies with labour worries. With industry flourishing and huge dividends almost a matter of course, the whole of industrial India in 1920 was ripe for a siege of unrest. Tata shares, leading the rest, rising or falling as much as 200 or 300 rupees in a single session of the exchange. Preferred went from its par of thirty rupees to a high of 1900. Cotton shares followed close behind Tata's. The Bombay mills were making new millionaires every week. But the cotton-mill operators still worked for starvation wages, still lived in horrible barracks, sometimes whole families of them jammed into one room. And it was early in 1920, before that first strike, that the Tata management made its big mistake, a blunder of omission which underlay the strike and a lot of subsequent misunderstandings.

Over a period of years the Tata workmen had received only one meagre raise, a 10 per cent increase in 1917. When the war ended the men began to worry about being cut again. Andrew Carnegie once said that every strike can be traced to negligence on the part of capital and management. It was so in this case. Had the Tata American management told the men frankly that they did not intend to withdraw that 10 per cent war bonus, but in fact planned to add a further 10 per cent raise, there never would have been any strike. And the management could have done so. For if the entire amount had come entirely from the holders of deferred shares only, which of course it would not have done, they would still have got a thirty-five rupee dividend, or well over 100 per cent on their original investment. The Tata management was at Jamshedpur, in direct contact with the men; the agents and directors of the company were over 1,000 miles away in Bombay. But the management was blind to the trends of the times, and the company paid dearly for their myopia.

There was no lack of indications to inform them. A group of anarchists, called the Terrorists, were making their opposition to the Government, to any Government, strongly felt in Bengal.

More important, through the Soviet consulates in Kandahar and Jalalabad in Afghanistan, near the Indian border, Russian literature filtered steadily into the country. Its philosophy was to stir up the masses first and later let the masses manage their own Government. Pictures were circulated, showing on one side a family of half-starved Russian peasants standing in front of a dilapidated cowshed, with a caption of *Under the Rule of the Tyrants*. On the other side a happy, robust family were seated before a model farmhouse with large barns, tractors, and other farm machinery in the background. The legend under this half read *The People Supreme,* and both titles were written in Hindi and Urdu.

While the decade of industrial revolution in India which commenced in 1920 resembled the industrial rebellion in England, it differed from it in one fundamental: the English Parliament in 1825 passed laws to suppress the awakening labour forces, in India the politicians and liberals did everything they could to improve the conditions of the labour classes. Naturally the thinking people of India were well aware of labour's power in England and of the history of its long struggle for recognition—doubly so because of the precedent provided.

Not until 1870 was it legal in England for any two or more men to agree jointly, or to conspire to act "in restraint of trade", unless such an act should be one punishable in an individual. The Parliament also legalized peaceful picketing. The working-man's liaison with the fecund wench, Progress, and their offspring, the trade-union movement, were thus made legitimate. In 1892 there were a million and a half labour union members. By 1926 the membership had increased to over five million. The Labour Party had come into political power and could write on its rolls the name of one Prime Minister.

In 1920, which was in so many ways a pivotal year for India, Indian labour found itself in the same position that English labour had occupied a century before. There was a big field for the politically ambitious, for, too, the hundreds of enlightened men who were deeply concerned with the betterment of the masses and walling, if necessary, to give their lives to that end. The improvement of the poor man's lot which came along in England with the growing strength of the labour movement was a goal for the Indian people to work towards. Such a powerful weapon must be in the hands of right-thinking men. And there were many such, who now devoted their waking moments to organizing labour, to helping the poor, towards freeing the peasants from their land poverty.

Tata's policy of care for the workman's welfare had always followed the benevolent principles first laid down by Jamshedjee Tata and held with equal conviction by his family. Every year new living quarters replaced some of the old accommodation, sometimes as many as 600 buildings in one year. In nearly all of them electric light and running water were installed. A worker could rent one of these brick and concrete dwellings for 2 or 3 per cent of the capital cost a year.

In the space set aside by Tata's for markets and bazaars a hundred or so shopkeepers had taken stalls from which they supplied the town residents with staple foods. But the market dealers were inclined to profiteer, especially when they dealt with the employees on a credit basis. Occasionally a rupee would buy only 10 lb. of rice. And rice is India's principal article of food. Also, other prices advanced in proportion.

Tata's built a huge grain store, bought rice by the trainload, and sold the rice to the workmen at gross cost, something like

20 lb. for a rupee. The bazaar dealers promptly dropped their prices and the workers saved money, which was tantamount to a wage increase. It was the same with the houses. The newly employed and the overflow people often lived in places owned by contractors or speculators, paying three times as much for a mud hut with a thatched roof, or a corrugated sheet-iron, one-room shack without running water, as their fellows paid for the comfortable company houses. As soon as possible, they were moved into the modern quarters and saved 75 per cent on their rental.

Much of the meaning of these measures went unnoticed by the majority of the workmen, who, like labourers everywhere, were more concerned with their nominal wage than their real wage. As employers well know, workmen will rush to high-wage areas, forgetting that while their pay envelopes are fat, they are paying more to live and are therefore saving less. They plan to raise their real wage as a rule by practising economy, and some of them do. But any forced saving or planned frugality is often resented as an infringement of personal liberty. This reaction was not uncommon in 1920 among the illiterate Indians in Jamshedpur to Tata's provident fund in which membership was compulsory for all employees other than foreign contract men. One half of one month's wages was deducted from a man's yearly earning, divided in twelve instalments. To this amount the company added the equivalent of a month's pay, and paid him 5 per cent interest on the whole. In times of need, the employee could always borrow from the fund at the normal rate of interest, perhaps 3 or 4 per cent, whereas a moneylender would have charged him from 50 to 100 per cent. In fact, such usurious rates are still being paid in parts of native States in India by poor workmen and farmers.

I have seen a moneylender's promissory note made out on a piece of palm leaf, the words burned into the fibre with a red-hot steel nib. The note was for fifteen rupees, but because of the high discount rates, the farmer received only about ten rupees. The interest payment specified was six rupees a year until the full amount of the note could be paid in a lump sum. When the farmer had paid out forty-eight rupees in interest, he defaulted and had to serve three years as a bonded labourer. Only then did the moneylender make a V-shaped cut on the palm leaf and free the borrower from debt. This was not an unusual case, although it could not happen in British India.

Even apparently satisfied workers can be affected by labour unrest. To follow the crowd and to get more while the getting is good is, after all, only human nature. And grain stores, provident funds, wholesome quarters, the highest wages in India, free hospitals, and free schools were forgotten by the Tata workmen under the influence of the widespreading disaffection, and of their own apprehension over a possible loss of their war bonus.

When the first labour union was formed in Jamshedpur after the 1920 strike, the committee was drawn largely from among the clerical staff, who in turn came principally from Bengal or Madras, so that many of our 5,000 up-country Punjabis refused to accept the union. A membership of 10,000 was claimed, but actually only about 1,500 men belonged, and they paid their dues fairly irregularly. Since it was far from being representative, the union was denied recognition until 1925, when Mahatma Gandhi, Motilal Nehru, the father of Jawaharlal, and C. F. Andrews came to Jamshedpur and discussed the matter with R. D. Tata and the new general manager, Charles A. Alexander, a Pennsylvanian. As a result, the company agreed to deal with the men through the union as long as it worked along constitutional lines as practised in the steel trade in England.

Mahatma Gandhi's friend, later his biographer, C. F. Andrews, chosen first president of the steel workers' union, was one of the finest men I have ever known and the indefatigable friend of labour. He did his best to get good men for local leaders. He never hesitated to tell his committee they were growing up too slowly, or if the men had a real grievance, to persist until the management swung round to his viewpoint. He saw that Tata's was more than an industry, it was a national asset. He imbued the men with the same spirit and turned them back into a crowd working for their own and the country's good as much as for their wages.

Thus, five years after a strike which had been engineered by outsiders, some of whom cared nothing for labour, collective bargaining was won for the workmen by India's greatest patriot, Mohandas Gandhi.

One reason that the local Tata management at Jamshedpur had been so blind to the necessity for change in their relations with the workmen was that as a group they were too much taken up with resisting every step in what we called Perin's "greater extensions".

The Tata Iron and Steel Company as it stands today gave free medical treatment to a million and a quarter patients in 1940 and paid its employees three and a half months' salary as bonus; further, it produced a million and a quarter tons of pig-iron and more than a million tons of steel ingots in the same year at costs lower than Perin ever predicted. None of this would have been possible without Perin, or without the Tata faith in him. But as far back as 1916, when Perin enlarged the two original blast furnaces from 12-foot to 14-foot 8-inch hearths, the local management at Jamshedpur insisted to the directors in Bombay that Perin was bound to ruin the company. "Let well enough alone", they chorused. Indian coal, they said, would never make a coke hard enough to stand up to requirements of larger-hearth blast furnaces.

And if Tata's wanted more pig-iron, they should build a number of small blast furnaces. One proposal from Jamshedpur suggested a string of cute little furnaces, 200-tons-a-day jobs, stretched across country like buttons on a typewriter.

Looking back on those years, I marvel that the plant continued to exist, much less to grow. Although the enlarged furnaces did actually produce 300 tons a day, they required more care and, bucking and rearing, kept the furnace men on their toes. The management was smug. "We told you so", they said. "Indian coke is just not good enough for large furnaces." And they condemned the furnaces—only to have their ears slapped back by the directors in Bombay. From then on the Jamshedpur clique opposed every Perin proposal as hare-brained. It was war to the bitter end, a war that cost Tata's millions of dollars. The management carried their animus so far that any man having the temerity to side openly with Perin was immediately dismissed.

One day in 1916 Perin stopped in the cast-house for a chat. He was designing two furnaces in New York, he said, which would have 17-foot hearths. Then he added, "Jack, if you'll spend less of your spare time trying to be a famous gentleman rider and more time concentrating on a furnace that will give us 1,000 tons a day, you'll see the time when such a tonnage is only what you expect of your furnace every twenty-four hours."

"What about the quality of our coke?" I asked.

"I'm planning to screen all the coal, and even to wash some of it", he answered. "And I'm going to build better coke-ovens. You know the American, Louis Wilputte? Well, he is designing new batteries of coke-ovens which will revolutionize blast furnace practice here", he went on. "When the new 450-ton furnaces commence averaging 600 tons a day, then go after the 1,000-ton furnace. You'll get it."

That was like Perin. As soon as one goal was achieved, he urged for a higher one. He was always seeking, never satisfied or complacent. While he was visualizing such tonnages in 1916, you could count on your fingers the blast furnaces in America which could average 500 tons a day for any length of time. Perin lived to see a furnace produce 36,000 tons in one month.

The two new 17-foot-hearth blast furnaces, fed with fine-quality coke by the new Wilputte ovens, did exactly what Perin had claimed they would, producing around 600 tons of iron a day apiece. And instead of requiring 2,800 lb. of coke for a ton of iron, they operated on 2,300 lb. of fuel per ton. One would have thought that at last the old nightmare of big furnaces would have vanished from the bogey-ridden minds of the management, but to speak of increasing the hearth diameter still further in their hearing was equivalent to resigning. Perin was working with high-grade Indian ore and coke containing 24 per cent ash, and producing more iron per day per furnace than the U.S. furnaces were doing then with high-grade fuel containing only 12 per cent ash, and a somewhat lower grade of ore.

But no. When only a very few years later the old blast furnace Perin had brought from Alabama during the war for ferro-manganese production was ready for the scrap-heap, the new furnace erected by the management in its place was not a 17-foot-hearth job—it was a small 14-foot-8-inch one. Their excuse was that a larger furnace would have been too great a capital investment, as the hot blast-stoves would have needed rebuilding. And that they wanted a furnace suitable for ferro-manganese. It was pretty obvious that they could have used one of the two small-hearth furnaces they already had for ferro. They built the small furnace out of spite for Perin, and threw another few million dollars down the flue in the doing.

Labour troubles and internecine war, coming as near as they did to dismembering the stripling steel company, were not the only hazards of those years. There was also the Gorgon of rising costs. Cost rises began in 1917 and continued every year in defiance of higher production. The cost of ore and fluxes consumed in the pig-iron furnaces did not increase, and the cost of labour per ton of pig-iron was nearly stationary. It was coal that went up and up, and then still higher, sending up the price of pig-iron and therefore of steel ingots and finished steel products. Of course, the Jamshedpur management pointed to the fact that a ton of pig-iron cost 100 per cent more to produce in 1923 than it had in 1917 as the clinching argument against Perin's extensions.

Until 1917, Tata's could buy their coal on the open market, picking and choosing what they wanted for their coke-ovens, stipulating best-quality, low-ash fuel. And there was plenty of it. Coal could be bought at the mines for three rupees per ton for years. But with the prosperity of the company and the pouring out of huge dividends to Tata shareholders in 1917, several old and reputable British firms decided to cut in on the industry and make Tata's pay all the market would stand for their coal supplies until they themselves wanted the collieries for projected steel works. And indeed, shortly after, some five British companies were floated for the making of steel. Only one became a reality, and then merely as a producer of pig-iron. But their activity meant that vast mining areas and millions of tons of ore were tied up subject to their demand.

The far-sighted Perin determined to protect his future steel production by acquiring a few first-class coal mines, even if he had to pay through the nose for them. He reckoned a future need for an additional 1,000,000 tons a year. The significance of this estimate was not lost on the British vested interests who owned many of the better collieries. When Perin started going after long-term leases, many owners offered to sell coking coal on a sliding scale, at from eight to sixteen cents a ton above the price paid by the Railway Board for first-class coal. Since the railroads bought what they needed every year on public tender, this proposition seemed reasonable enough.

Colliery owners were more or less indifferent as long as Tata's required only half a million tons a year, but with the prospect of' tripled demand that might again be increased, the interested British business men forming the coal ring seemed to act with the unformulated and tacit purpose of making Tata's pay the limit. Because of the war, which kept a lot of the Welsh coal out of Eastern ports, they did a big business in bunkering ships from world ports. And, with the price of bunker coal thereby going up, the ring could now afford to tender high prices for railway coal. The more the railways paid for coal, the higher the cost to Tata's on the new long-term contracts. Don't forget that, in 1917, 3,000 lb. of coke went up in smoke for every ton of pig-iron produced.

By 1923 Tata's were using only 2,300 gross lb. per ton, which was not bad, with coke containing 24 per cent ash, and which had a carbon content of 75 per cent compared to 87 per cent in the U.S. In that same year Tata's were able to supply a large percentage of their own coal for the coke-ovens and to tender also for big quantities of coal for the use of the railways. Almost at once the price of pig-iron began to drop. Still, just then, when the new plant was ready for operation, it cost Tata's 125 rupees to make a ton of rails on the old mills, the same rails for which the railways paid exactly 125 rupees. As old Blaser said wryly, "At least we're not selling the rails at a loss".

One of the less admirable British type in India, in other words a diehard, once told me with some satisfaction that India's industrial activity would soon collapse. Steel and other manufacturing depended on coal for their initial power supply. Since he had been informed that India's known coking coal would be nearly exhausted by the year 2025, the country's vast iron ore reserves would then be available for British rather than Indian use. India would never be able to import coal and compete with the old country.

I am not a diehard, and I say that long before India has scratched the bottom of her collieries she will have harnessed the Himalayas, her God-given protection on the north, to furnish all the hydroelectric power she needs for her steel and other industries. Low-grade coal will merely supply the carbon for reducing iron ore; electric power will provide the heat units.

The "practical" engineer will laugh me down, because of the tremendous cost of transmitting current over such a distance. But practical engineers forty years ago would have scoffed at the mere idea of present transmission lines, and did, before that, jeer at Cecil Rhodes and his suggestion of overland transport from Cape Town to Cairo. Tata electric companies have already strung the western hills of India with cables which carry cheap power to the Bombay side. I don't know what would prevent them from developing the Himalayas. Giant generators, power lines above or below the surface, power measured in millions of volts instead of thousands—why not?

When our American Mesabi range iron deposits are exhausted, as they will be in about fifty years, I doubt that the United States will remain a steel-producing country. But if she does, she will depend increasingly on imported ores. Personally, I think that soon steel will be supplanted by some alloy, like that of magnesium aluminium. Some metallurgists of repute told me a few years ago that metallic sections of this alloy weigh less than half as much as steel sections and are twice as strong. If the United States does stay in the steel business, however, the plants of the future will be built along the eastern seaboard, as they were in the old charcoal-burning days. Iron ore will be worth more a century hence, and it will pay steel men to ship it up from Cuba, Brazil—and from India.

From the Indian point of view, shipping iron ore out of the country to be made into steel elsewhere for the sake of big and quick profits would be a very short-sighted policy. Anyone who has travelled in India has been carried over rails marked "Made by the Carnegie Steel Company, U.S.A." If India is wise enough to protect and further her steel industry, Americans some day may ride over rails right in their own country stamped "Made in India".

CHAPTER VI

TERRORISTS ARE BRITISH STEPCHILDREN

STEEL, AS VITAL a factor as gold in a country's peace-time strength, is an even more powerful weapon of war. Every Government restricts the sale and export of steel at the first hint of impending conflict. Its value rises and its price sky-rockets. Every Government, too, which has the resources, does its damnedest to bring steel output to ever-higher peaks in the shortest possible time.

In the first World War, Germany planned her initial attacks so as to secure for herself the coal- and iron-fields of Belgium, Northern France, and Poland. By doing so she raised the steel production of the Central Powers from 21,000,000 tons (compared to the Allies' 19,000,000) to 24,000,000 tons, in the space of a few weeks, and reduced the Allied output proportionately. Only when the intervention of the United States brought Allied production up to 58,000,000 tons was the war lost for the Kaiser.

In preparing for the second World War, Germany stepped up her steel production until in 1938, the last year of peace, she was producing 22,991,000 tons, or more than Great Britain and France combined. Russia also had made great industrial progress, greater than any of us knew, as proved by her annual production of 18,156,000 tons in 1938, compared to a mere 4,436,000 at the start of the first World War. Iron Age for March, 1943, gives U.S. figures as 52,000,000 tons in 1939, 82,930,000 tons in 1941, and, by the end of 1942, 89,000,000 tons, or almost double that of all the Axis countries put together.

Now, in the early 1920's, at the beginning of what we thought of then as the peace, India had proved what she could do in war-time output of steel, starting nearly from scratch and reaching an annual average of 300,000 tons. Yet it looked very much as though she were going to lose that great new asset which promised so much for the future, to be thrown back to the pre-capitalistic era of the ploughshare and the hand-loom. India and the civilization of her awakening masses were unsafe until she could attain and continue production of at least the total quantity of steel needed for her transport systems and her manufactures.

Although at this time the steel industries of the other producers, England, Germany, the United States, and France, were in bad straits, any one of them could easily have wiped out the infant Indian industry in their struggle for new markets. Various trade letters from our London office sketched the conditions in England during 1922-1923, when Tata's extensions were finished and ready for use.

One report says, "Makers are sacrificing all profits, selling often even at a loss to get orders. But still they have neither been able to keep their plants running continuously, nor to stimulate demand by rolling at a loss." According to another: "British steel-makers are so eager to avoid shutting down altogether that they take export orders at a pound or two below the prevailing selling price in England."

The chairman of one company, addressing the shareholders, said there was no steel-works in England that was making ends meet. Their own production had reached a record of 160,000 tons of ingots, but they brought only £1,110,000, whereas in 1921, with a make of but 150,000 tons, the sales amounted to £2,700,000. "I don't believe any works in Great Britain can produce rolled steel, bars, sectional steel, or rails, at less than £8, which I believe to be ten shillings below cost. Recently the South African Government placed an order for 3,000 tons of rails, and paid £7 12*s*. 3*d*. per ton f.o.b. Liverpool. The cost of those, rails delivered from the Workington mill to f.o.b. Liverpool could not be less than twelve and a half shillings a ton, having a net of £7 f.o.b. works. On the other hand, the same works sold several thousand tons of rails to an English railway, receiving, according to my information, £9 ex-works. I think that some of the works which have taken unremunerative figures for the sentimental satisfaction of keeping going will probably not be able to carry on after the end of this year."

In this same year nearly every country erected tariff barriers against imports, especially against countries with devaluated currencies and those which were dumping steel products. For instance, in the case of German goods exported to Canada worth 1,000 marks, or about $20 at the current rate of exchange, the duty was payable at not less than $120. Australia not only raised tariff walls, but paid bounties on home production.

New Zealand set aside £150,000 a year for payment of twelve shillings a ton bounty on pig-iron, puddled bar iron, and steel produced from bar iron, and twenty-four shillings per ton for steel from the furnaces in New Zealand. South Africa drew up a Scheme to protect its still unborn iron and steel industry. British Columbia paid bounties on native pig-iron. France enacted a duty of 360 francs per ton. Belgium protected its home industries against Germany and the other former enemy countries which had debased currencies. Even Spain, on November 26, 1920, in a royal decree, had placed high tariff walls against dumping by foreign countries.

Italy admitted machinery free of duty and of consumption taxes for five years. New industries were exempted from both profits taxes and surtaxes, with this result in Italy's production:

		1,900	1919
Pig-Iron	:	24,000 tons	239,710 tons
Steel ingots	:	115,000 "	731,800 "

Japan had long fostered her home industries. In 1917 she passed a law exempting everyone engaged in the steel industry from income and business taxes, and providing bounties for various domestic steel products. By 1921 the domestic production of steel had risen so that it equalled the steel imports in volume.

The United States raised the levy on steel sheets and bars from 12 to 20 per cent, with a resulting rise in production. Only India was unprotected. And everybody realized that here was a fine dumping ground. Two American firms opened offices in Calcutta and tried to edge in on the markets. Boatloads of steel which were raffled off in Continental ports were sent to India and sold at ridiculous prices. During the year ending in March 1923, 916,083 tons of major steel bars, etc., were imported into India. From England 313,853 tons; from Belgium, 193,022 tons; from Germany, 74,008 tons; from Norway, 2,136 tons; from France, 3,590 tons; from Luxembourg, 6,038 tons; from U.S.A., 35,205 tons.

And a further 256,848 tons of steel products found their way into Indian ports in the form of railway sleepers, wire, bolts, nuts, cables, and bridge materials. Even 490 tons of steel-sheet rice bowls came in in one year!

All this gives a pretty fair picture of world steel-trade conditions on the eve of our blowing in the first new furnace to launch the greater extensions. Without protection from unfair competition, the company would undoubtedly have died, and in dying have left behind an India in a state of panic, in despair of becoming an industrial nation, left with only its fields and its crops. I don't think it is an exaggeration to say that the failure of Tata's would have set India back centuries in her development.

British vested interests looked upon India as a consumer of their home products. They certainly did not want Indian competition. The original Tata plant built by Perin didn't worry them much. But the greater extensions threatened to close to them a profitable market, especially since Tata's were planning to produce galvanized sheets to supplant the 300,000 tons imported every year. Two completely dissimilar factors, by the way, caused the steady demand for galvanized sheets in India: earthquakes and monkeys.

In Indian districts subject to frequent earthquakes, brick houses are dangerous, cracking open at the least tremor. Assam seems to be the worst sufferer, undoubtedly because the Himalayas have not yet settled down and may not assume their permanent shape for the next hundred million years. Decades ago, some enterprising natives, tired of eternally rebuilding their brick dwellings, experimented with bamboo houses, using galvanized-iron sheets for walls and roofs on this resilient framework. Soon the province was dotted with steel houses. Assam and eastern Bengal use more than 100,000 tons of sheets every year.

As for the monkeys, many rural districts, notably in the south of India, are infested with great tribes of them, living undisturbed in the village trees. These little devils are great thieves and vandals, but no one would think of doing them any harm, although the villagers fervently wish they would migrate elsewhere. I have even heard of forced migrations near the Tata works.

Some sixty miles down the railway from us, grain dealers were complaining bitterly of the depredations of monkeys, which raided grain-storage godowns near the station. They swarmed in through any door left open on a freight train and played havoc with the grain.

The damage and loss became so great that the railroad began running regular monkey trains. A locomotive would pull a dozen freight-cars onto a siding. Plenty of grain was then strewn on the car floors, and a door on each side left open. In no time at all hundreds of monkeys would fill the cars and begin stuffing themselves. The doors would be closed tightly and the train would run several miles down the track. As soon as it stopped and the doors were opened, out would jump the monkeys, chattering and screaming, no doubt swearing a blue streak in their own language. But either the tourist monkeys went right back, or others immediately took their places. Anyway, it didn't pay to continue the monkey excursions. I don't remember how the harassed grain dealers solved their problem—if they ever did.

Monkeys continually hunt vermin. And vermin like to live in straw roofs. Monkeys have therefore hunted their crawling prey on straw roofs ever since there were such things. It took only a few days' energetic hunting to make great holes in the thatched roofs of native huts. As soon as the monsoons started, the natives inside were deluged with rain-water. Some inventive Indian built a mud hut, roofed it with tin sheets, and then covered the tin with thatching to keep the house cool during the hot season. The monkeys still made holes in the thatch, but they couldn't penetrate the tin. The first such roofing was made of old kerosene tins flattened out. Then some brilliant fellow bought galvanized sheets and opened up a market for hundreds of thousands of tons of them. The steel industry of India is thus indebted to the native monkeys for a large and lucrative outlet for one of its products.

If the English industrialists regarded India solely as a field for their exploitation, the empire-builders and the Indian Government took a much longer view. Empire-builders in general are apt to feel that the empire is a polyglot of countries bound tightly to the mother country by the empire's life-line; Gibraltar, Malta, and Port Said; Suez and Aden; Bombay, Calcutta, and Colombo; Singapore and Hongkong; Melbourne and Vancouver; Montreal, Halifax-—and back to Liverpool. There stretches the traditional chain of empire. The Tata Company, flexing the adolescent muscles of industrial India, had sent steel flowing from Indian ports to strengthen that chain. Whether or not the empire-builders could foresee how vital Indian steel would be when Germany and Japan were doing all they could to demolish the life-line and had indeed forcibly removed some of its links, the Government did take steps to protect its continued production. And having made the first move, the Government turned its attention to other industries, old and new, to the irrigation of desert tracts and their cultivation with modern agricultural implements, to the damming up of rivers to provide electric power for further industrialization.

When the tariff walls were being discussed, there were many Indians who sided with the British diehard industrialists, although for a different reason. Their contention was that eventually the consumer would have to pay the higher cost. And why, they said, should the Government place a high duty on imported galvanized sheets when Tata's had not yet produced a single ton of them?

The answer is that at that time the sheet trade in India was a monopoly, with a few British firms importing practically all galvanized sheets, principally from Wales and the Tees-side. The profits were exorbitant. But under a protective tariff, production increased 1,500 per cent in the Tata plant alone; conversely, production cost dropped from 320 rupees a ton in 1924 to 110 rupees in 1937. When they cost 320 rupees, Indians had to pay 350 rupees a ton for galvanized sheets; today, with a nominal duty in effect, Indians can buy them for 160 rupees, because Tata is producing all they need.

The argument for high protective duties goes back beyond the first World War. The figures following came from Professor Taussig of Harvard University and were presented by us to the Indian Tariff Board in 1923. The significant factor is that during the period covered, Germany and the U.S. had high tariffs, England had none:

	Great Britain	*U.S.A.*	*Germany*
1870 . .	5,963,000 tons	1,665,000	1,391,000
1880 . .	7,749,000 „	3.835,000	2,729,000
1890 . .	7,904,000 „	9,203,000	4,658,000
1900 . .	8,960,000 „	13,789,000	8,348,000
1910 . .	10,012,000 „	27,304,000	14,556,000

These tonnages are for pig-iron. Since nearly 95 per cent of the pig-iron produced in these countries is converted into steel, obviously steel production increased proportionately.

From the figures we can see that Great Britain, with her free-trade policy, possessing an enormous initial advantage in having an established industry, and, aided by her control of world markets and freights, had by 1910 increased production less than 100 per cent. But in the U.S.A., which used tariff walls to foster industry, production went up more than 1,000 per cent.

A large part of the tremendous debt to American firms which Tata's had contracted in building the greater extensions was owed to the General Electric Company. They seemed, however, to worry less about getting their money than Tata's did about paying it. We seldom had a complaint on a piece of General Electric equipment, but whenever we did, the machinery was replaced promptly and without question. They almost spoiled us. We often required a turbine to run at a 25 per cent overload for months, and gradually came to believe that a generator or a turbo blower wasn't any good if it couldn't run at peak or even overload for a considerable time. G.E. not only supplied excellent equipment, they went out of their way to train Indians in their American plants so that the men could go back to India and operate machinery expertly, perhaps for a competitor. The company maintained a staff of engineers in Calcutta who were always ready to come out to Jamshedpur, men who were trained in steam-unit and rolling-mill operation as well as in electrical-installations work. The present Tata chief electrical engineer is a former General Electric man.

George Westinghouse had been one of Jamshedjee Tata's hosts in America at the end of the last century. After George's death, his company took any employee of Tata's, executive or student, under its wing whenever we were outside of India. One of the most interesting men I know worked in the General Electric office in Paris. Louis took me to dine one night at a little out-of-the-way place quite different from the big restaurants I, like most Americans, had patronized. He introduced me to the chef and owner, who prepared a very special dinner for us. He sat down with us from time to time while we were feasting, and I gathered that my friend Louis was something of a hero in his eyes. Turning to me, he asked if Louis had ever told me of the part he had played in an early-morning shooting party during the World War. Louis had to be coaxed to talk about it.

The "shooting party" was actually the execution of a woman spy. A closed carriage drove up to the appointed place. The prisoner stepped out, took a few steps, and stumbled. A soldier offered her his arm. Pointing to her high heels, the woman said quietly, "It is nothing. I am ready." One minute later at least nine bullets had pierced her body. An officer then emptied his revolver into her head. The body which lay inert in the courtyard was that of Mata Hari.

Like many others, I had heard that at the last moment Mata Hari had cast aside her cloak and stood forth in all her naked loveliness. Louis remarked dryly that the last time he saw her, along the sight of his rifle barrel, she had been fully clothed. He added that there had been nothing dramatic about the execution. I asked him what he had thought of when he pulled the trigger. He replied, "She was responsible for the deaths of thousands of Frenchmen. I thought of those French soldiers, of how they could never be avenged, not by killing a hundred Mata Haris."

I remember another story of the first World War. This one concerns B. P. Padshah, and took place in India. Or rather it starts with Padshah's failure to find in Bombay two books he wanted which had just been published, and involves the assistant superintendent of the blast furnaces, whom we called Little Bull. Little Bull was in Calcutta, where he had a couple of good things on the races. I sent him a wire saying, "Go Spinks Get Tarzan Apes Return Tarzan."

It was war-time and all telegrams were censored. The C.I.D. pricked up their ears. Here was a wire coming from a big munitions centre which, since it made no appreciable sense to them, might be in code. Immediately they cornered Little Bull at the Great Eastern Hotel and, showing him the wire, demanded to know what it meant. Little Bull flew into a rage and told them to go to hell, he didn't know anything about any man named Spinks, or Tarzan, or anything about any damned ape. And he added a few of his more inventive adjectives. The C.I.D. appreciated his flow of language so much they placed him under partial arrest. He was forbidden to leave the hotel, much less to go to the track. Little Bull was fit to be tied.

It was all cleared up when the C.I.D. men went in to Spinks', the bookseller's, with my enigmatic message. The salesman took one look at it and handed them the two volumes required. Little Bull was released, still fuming. He threatened to go to the American Consul and declare war on England.

If it served no other purpose, that incident was, at any rate, proof of the vigilance of the C.I.D. The very patient attention to detail which characterizes the C.I.D. in India removes from possibility any such widespread, master-minded terrorist group as most travellers in the East are told make the I.R.A. in Ireland, or the old Sicilian Black Hand, look like sportive youngsters. The travellers usually believe what they're told, and in the retelling invariably add a little something of their own. The Government crowd can only benefit from the theory that they have constantly to contend with a powerful secret society of violent anarchists. And so the myth grows.

I once met a woman who was typical of the average voyager to India. We both sat at the chief engineer's table on an old B.I. steamer between Hongkong and Singapore. This woman had been born in Arlington, Massachusetts, but, like many expatriates, was anxious to be known by her husband's nationality, which was Canadian, rather than by her own. One day the conversation turned to the comparative merits of Indian and Chinese teas. She was the sort of person who would say to the chief engineer, "Speaking of tea, didn't the revolt of the American colonies have something to do with the dumping of some tea? I seem to vaguely remember reading about it when I was a little girl."

So naturally, when she asked questions about India, the chief handed her some tall yarns. Once she remarked that the terrorist party in India, called the Thugs, must be connected with the infamous thugs of America's big cities—after all, they had the same name. The chief winked at me and then spun her a long tale about some uncle of his having come close to death at the hands of Thugs years before. That afternoon, lying in my deck chair, I heard that expatriate telling the story to someone else, only now it was undoubtedly true because the victim was her uncle. For good measure she added that the Thugs had become so wealthy they were sending their sons abroad to Oxford and Cambridge to be educated. I felt sorry for her, and later put her straight about the Thugs. I guess I, too, wanted to show off my knowledge.

The Thugs were organized bands of assassins who once travelled in fairly large numbers throughout India. They worshipped Kali, the Hindu goddess of destruction, and strangely enough some of them were at the same time Mohammedans. They spoke in a patois of their own, and used certain signs to make themselves known to each other, much as members of Western secret societies do. It was their rule to kill only at dawn, first performing a certain ritual, and then strangling the victim with a noose. If the prisoner survived one dawn, he was safe until the next.

All this was a long time ago, during the time when Lord William Bentinck was Governor-General of India, 1828-1835. It was he who decided to have no more nonsense with Thugs, arrested some 1,600 of them, hanged 400, and sent the rest into exile on the Andaman Islands. While there were still a few Thugs around as late as 1850, undoubtedly this tribe of fanatics is now extinct. Legends about them are kept alive in the minds of the credulous, to their own consequent mixed delight and terror. But after twenty-five years of daily contact with various strata of the Indian population, I am convinced that there is no master mind behind the terrorist movement in India—that is, outside the heads of the propagandist and the fiction writer.

No, the binding cement among terrorists is a desire to overthrow the British Raj in India, and it ties together in a common cause thousands of men who don't even know one another. While their theory that murder of innocent officials will at once stir up the Indians and attract sympathy for the cause from America and Europe may be open to question, they have the Irish terrorists as a shining example. People soon forget the poor officials murdered in Ireland and turn their sympathy towards the murderer. As soon as he is hanged he becomes a patriotic martyr.

In my opinion the terrorist's theory is wrong, at the very least as regards the reaction of the outside world. One British official dies and the British papers feature the story for weeks. Former assassinations are recalled to fill out a picture of complete Indian lawlessness. Public indignation is aroused and the layman led to believe that India is indeed far from fit for Home Rule. The seed of the Indian terrorist ripens in the contradictions of British diehard psychology.

Every year until the present war began, nearly 20,000 young Indians returned to their native land from English, European, and American universities with degrees in law, medicine, and the arts. The comparatively small number of students who came back equipped for technical work fared better than their fellows specializing in the professions. The young doctors and lawyers looked about for work in suitable jobs. But whereas a mechanic who had never been near a college could get a job with a starting pay of a dollar a day and work up in a few years to three or four times - that much, the want-ad columns of any Indian paper offered, for instance, a permanent post to a qualified doctor on a tea plantation beginning at $20 a month and rising by yearly increases of a dollar a month to a maximum pay of $40 ! And—there would be hundreds of applicants for the job. We have advertised two or three times for a junior doctor for our hospital, where the pay was much higher. We always had more than 2,000 applications, some of them from Edinburgh and London graduates.

If the young Indian doctors were in bad case, they were no worse off than the neophyte' lawyers, for whom the obvious and desirable place would, of course, have been Government service. But seldom was there a vacancy. Tom from Cheltenham, Dick from Surrey, and Harry from Winchester, all of whom were college friends of the Indian aspirants, had promptly plucked what Government plums there were. Furthermore, this particular type of Britisher seems to have an extremely faulty memory. I have seen some instances in India, and heard of many more, in which the flowers of the English public-school system, become bureaucrats, have barely been able to remember the acquaintanceship, and that with unmistakable condescension. My wife and I even experienced one such expert snubbing.

We were at the Viceroy's ball one year when Lord Halifax held the office. The ballroom was the great hall of Belvedere, whose walls were lined with portraits, where Clive and Hastings had often led cotillions, where Madame de Talleyrand had once held all eyes with her beauty. We were both pleasurably aware that we were treading on ground made historical by the deeds and the misdeeds of many of the people who had known this room before us. The floor where we were trying to dance was; crowded. Between dances we saw a couple we knew, an engineer, and his wife, who was the daughter of an English Lord. I had known and done business with the man for years. He had several times been a guest in my house. I smiled and greeted the man. He looked at me blankly, gave me a curt nod, and passed on. To our surprise, we had been cut dead.

At a dinner-party in Jamshedpur the previous week I had given Lady Halifax my selections for the Viceroy's Cup, which was to be run the day after the ball, writing them down on the back of her place-card for reference. She backed all three horses to place, or, as we would say in the United States, to place and show, and won on each of them. After the races my wife and I went to a garden-party. Lady Halifax came over to talk with us and to compliment me on my knowledge of horseflesh. The Bishop of Calcutta was also in the group.

Just then the same engineer fellow came by and realized at a glance that apparently we passed muster socially. As soon as Lady Halifax and an A.D.C. had joined some other people, he came rushing over, effervescing with friendliness. "You must come to us for luncheon tomorrow," he said. "We won't take no for an answer."

We said politely that we had another engagement. We were urged to set our own date. We regretted, but we were booked up. That was the only time I have seen my wife's gentle blue eyes flash. And I can't say I blame her.

One must know the average Englishman of India to understand the educated young Indian's point of view, for the Englishman of India is quite different from the Englishman one meets in London. The English industrialist or engineer—in fact, nearly all Englishmen at home—are really fine fellows. But the British civil servant in India is more than likely an obnoxious snob, and not unlikely to be proud of it. It's not altogether his fault either. From being an Englishman among other Englishmen and comparatively a nobody at home, the young civil servant is suddenly transplanted, with some authority, to a country where he is a little god-almighty.

Not all civil servants are stinkers. Many civilians, particularly those who were born in India, start out by being admirable men in service. It's the boys who are doing their best to climb who give all the rest a bad name, because they're trying to uphold a completely false prestige. In many cases hard work and responsibility mellow them. They come finally to realize that they are, after all, only tax-gatherers and keepers of the peace.

Ironically enough, when they leave their own local dung-heaps and go to Calcutta or Bombay they feel very ordinary, since neither English nor Indian business men give them a second glance. For a few years they may dress for dinner when they are at their stations even if the dinner is served in a tent. But gradually they begin coming to table in khaki shorts and a shirt; they work far into the night making out reports, writing appeals for money for a few extra doctors for their district, or for a small school. They labour for the good of humanity, and when eventually they leave India they take with them the blessings of the people of their districts. India as a rule turns them into the finest type of men.

But long before that desirable change has taken place, most of these young, green British bureaucrats have met and snubbed Indians of their own age who were college friends, and for no reason except that they were Indians.

What is the effect of these rebuffs on the young Indians? Just what it would be on anybody else. He is affronted that people at whose homes he has been more than welcome, with whom he has had several years of intimate contact, are reluctant to acknowledge him on his own home ground. At first he is hurt to the quick. Then he is resentful. And from that resentment springs a deep and not unreasonable hatred.

Buffeted about, unable to pursue whatever profession he is fitted for, feeling menial work to be beneath him, he withdraws into himself and begins to brood. Soon he is excellent material for the first terrorist he meets. He is introduced to hashish and becomes an addict. Under its influence he comes to believe that at last he has a place, a useful function in life—to free his country. If he forfeits his life, he will at least have attained martyrdom. And there you have a new terrorist.

That process of reasoning explains why so few terrorists are brought to trial. They take their own lives by preference. Thus also is the identity of co-workers and directing minds, if any, preserved from exposure.

Candidates for political martyrdom in India are not always male. Two well-dressed young Bengali girls, not more than fourteen or fifteen, walked into a criminal court-room a few years ago and up to the bench where an English judge presided. Without doubt they didn't know that the judge was about to resign his post to make way for an Indian successor. But if they had, it probably wouldn't have made any difference, for there was nothing personal in their attitude or actions.

They bowed to the judge and he smiled in return. One of the girls handed him an envelope. As the magistrate reached out to take it, the other girl, not more than five feet away, shot him dead. Both conspirators were arrested. They refused to give evidence and were sent to the Andaman Islands. To this day they are considered heroines in Bengal.

Instead of exalting the criminals and offering sympathy to their families, however, true Indian patriots have long been horrified by such incidents. I have yet to meet an Indian who was not both shocked and ashamed at the crimes committed during the last twenty years by his young, drugged, misguided countrymen. No one suffers more real pain than Mohandas Gandhi. And the pain is all the more galling because the conditions which bring about violent terroristic acts are so unnecessary.

True patriots remember bitterly that in 1858 the good Queen Victoria took her Indian subjects to her heart, proclaiming that, *"It is Our further Will that, so far as may be, Our Subjects, of whatever Race or Creed, be freely and impartially admitted to Offices in Our Service, the Duties of which they may be qualified, by their education, ability, and integrity, duly to discharge."* Not unnaturally, that was taken to mean that there would be Indians in all subordinate Government posts, Indian superior court judges, Indian governors. Had the Queen's high purposes been carried out by all her ministers and viceroys instead of by a dogged, enlightened few, there would never have been any terrorists in India.

It is the British diehards who have fathered them, and who perpetuate terrorism by continuing to send younger sons out from Kent and Surrey and Ulster and Argyle to rule. If the Indian university graduate had his rightful chance to acquire training in the governing of his native land, he would ably demonstrate his good citizenship, his pride in membership of a great empire, his ability as an Indian to make and enforce the laws of India. Without recruits to draw from, terrorism would vanish. The lives of those desperate young men are wasted more tragically than if they faced death fairly on the field of battle.

So it is clear that there is no organized terroristic movement in India. Even if things were not as they are, I would be convinced that there could be no large, effective organization because of that very efficiency of the C.I.D. which led them to suspect possible danger in my cryptogram about Tarzan and his apes.

Investigators of the Criminal Investigation Department are usually as able as they are painstaking. Further, they command more constructive imagination than is traditionally credited to British Government servants. An educated young Indian from a village not far from Jamshedpur told me about the work of one of these men in solving a mystery which had thrown the whole tiny town into an uproar of fear and anger.

The body of a tribesman was found hanging from a tree some fifteen feet above the ground by a six-foot rope. The village chief dispatched a couple of runners to a distant police post, and a C.I.D. man who happened to be in the district responded.

By questioning he soon found that the dead man had been despondent over bad health and the loss of his oxen from plague. He then pointed out to the excited assemblage that if anyone had killed the man, the assailant would have had to carry his dead weight up into the tree, because of the shortness of the rope. Instead, he said, the man was a suicide. The villagers refused this simple explanation and continued to mill about him uneasily, talking murder and demanding that he find the killer.

Finding that line of reasoning too abstract for the people, the C.I.D. man quickly evolved another. He told an assistant to climb up to the same limb of the tree and fasten the rope, the other end of which he now tied about the neck of an onlooker. The man thought he was going to be murdered then and there and started shouting for help and making such a racket that hundreds of other villagers came rushing out of their houses to see what was up.

Raising his hand to silence the hubbub, the investigator said, "You have just seen it proved that the dead man was not murdered. Had he been attacked, he would certainly have yelled for help as our friend here did, and you would all have come running to help him, just as you did now. As there were no such cries for help, surely the man must have taken his own life."

No organization bent upon crime could exist very long without running foul of the Department. The sweeper in the mud hut which passes for a schoolroom, the coolie in a garage, a lathe hand in a railway workshop, a candy vendor in a bazaar, a football fan in a grandstand, a flunkey on a train—any and all of these may be members of the C.I.D. Half a dozen terrorists ganged together might get away with it, but even a slightly enlarged group would sooner or later be joined by a C.I.D. man. The band would be allowed to operate until they definitely incriminated themselves, then suddenly the police would swoop down upon the leaders and cart them off to prison without trial.

Such action is perfectly permissible under the Act of 1818, which was passed to protect witnesses against a man who is standing trial from inevitable extermination by the man's vengeful relatives. It has been compared in effect to the secret accusation box in the Palace of the Doges in Venice. All you have to do is to tell the police that a man is a terrorist and give a few relevant facts. The next thing you know the man has been arrested and is on his way to the Andaman Islands, even in 1940. This does not mean that the Indian Government would imprison a man without good reason, nor would it, like the Doges of Venice, act on the word of a person not known to its officials. The Government has at its service several thousand trained special policemen who act as informers.

Many lathe hands, dynamiter's helpers, sweepers, and others at Tata's are C.I.D. men. Tata's gargantuan plant is now a great national institution which produces an indispensable flow of war materials. It is also, or could be without ceaseless vigilance, an excellent place for terrorists to insinuate themselves and slyly to secure materials for their own private warfare.

I remember the story of a bomb. The story of the man who used it I do not know, for he gave his life in the same explosion which killed his hapless victims. The C.I.D. examined the only two pieces of the bomb which were recovered, embedded in the side of a house. These indicated that the bomb had been a home-made affair. C.I.D. men set out on a patient tracing of the one fragment and the sliver of steel inside it. The fragment had a square, slightly worn protrusion, plainly a nut, worn from many contacts with a wrench. It was found to be a cap for an oxygen cylinder. The curl of steel was a shaving which could have been made only by a powerful lathe, such a lathe as Tata's used for necking their rolls. Indeed, analysis showed that a certain metalloid used by Tata's in the composition of rolls identified the piece as having come from the big lathe in Tata's shop. It was noted that Tata's use about 20,000 cylinders of oxygen every month and have, in fact, an oxygen factory inside the works.

The C.I.D. sent to the Punjab for one of their expert machinists and lathe hands. As soon as a vacancy occurred this man was employed to work a lathe on the night shift. He became friendly with his fellow-workmen. He observed that the men on the night shift sometimes made things for themselves, such as knives with long sharp blades like daggers, and even longer knives like swords. One evening he saw a fellow putting threads on the end of a short piece of round steel. Shortly after, the same man was discovered to be cutting the threaded end off the bar. That threaded end made a fine plug for an oxygen cylinder cap.

The watchful C.I.D. operator noticed that one of the men was in the habit of visiting the chemical laboratory casually during the night. Soon the source of an explosive mixture was located, and by further persistence the Government worker learned that a box of fifty sticks of nitroglycerine had been, stolen from dynamiters who were blowing out the salamander of a blast furnace.

Still the C.I.D. took no action. In a week or so one of the night shift asked for leave and went off to Calcutta. The C.I.D. man was close on his heels, quite near enough to note the address of the house he entered in Kidderpur, a subdivision of Calcutta. The operator knew that a meeting was in progress in the house and that one of the plotters was an undercover man for the police department. The house was surrounded, the C.I.D. squad entered, found a large cache of bombs, and arrested the conspirators. One half of their prisoners were university graduates.

Some C.I.D. recruits work for the police instead of paying other, less productive, retribution to the State. Many of them have records. There was the case of D-2, a man whom I heard of first by accident.

Gin Bill and I were at a table in the Blood Tub a week or two before the 1922 strike. Next to us the general manager of Tata's and the assistant superintendent of police were talking, not too discreetly. Bill and I overheard the police official say, "I will have a talk with D-2. He ought to know the latest developments." I happened to see the police superintendent at the plant that afternoon. An employee passed him. Neither man spoke. The officer walked away. In a few minutes the employee followed. I had a good look at the man known as D-2.

Three days later at a giant mass meeting, when it was evident that a strike was coming, who should jump up on the platform and egg the workers on but D-2. He completely gained the confidence of the workmen with the fire of his eloquence as he urged them to strike. He did it too well. I heard later that D-2 had earned a severe reprimand for over-playing his part. I also heard his history from another C.I.D. man. D-2 had been arrested for murder some time before. Because there were extenuating circumstances he was sentenced only to life imprisonment. After six or seven years he was allowed to leave prison, a free man as far as anybody knew. But he was not free. He had to go wherever he was sent, to keep his eyes and ears open, and to report his findings. From then on D-2's freedom depended on his discretion and his ability.

Lack of discretion sent another C.I.D. man back to jail for good. For the sake of a mild irony, his name shall be A-1. A-1 was enamoured of the comely wife of a neighbour. The lady was apparently more than willing. A-1 conceived the charming idea of sending the husband somewhere else, where he wouldn't be in the way, say in jail. A-1 got hold of a number of seditious pamphlets and planted them in the neighbour's house. Then he informed on the man. The police duly raided the house, found the treasonous literature, and were about to arrest the husband when they noticed that each pamphlet bore a police mark and number. A-1 had filched the evidence from the desk of a clerk in the police station!

It was a neat case of the biter bitten. In his prison cell the amorous informer had plenty of time to ponder, not only the Ten Commandments, but a G.I.D. eleventh, *Thou shalt cover thy tracks.*

CHAPTER VII

INDIANIZATION OF TATA'S

I FIND MYSELF continually returning to the year 1920, which seems quite clearly to divide the old India from the new. It stands at the end of the period that started in 1858 with the quelling of the Indian mutiny.

Before 1920 many old customs were still current, even in the new iron and steel business. A workman could be discharged on the slightest provocation. He could be fined for not notifying his foreman that he was ill, although he might live five miles from the plant, without, of course, a telephone, and be suffering from a high fever.

In those days a department head walking about the plant would be followed by various youngsters. If it were the rainy season, one lad would carry the boss's raincoat and umbrella, others would bring up the procession with writing-pad, pen and ink, perhaps a tin of cigarettes. When the American or Continental department head was ready to leave, his *syce*, or groom, brought his carriage to the works gates and ran along behind as the white lord drove off. If the *syce* got caught stealing a ride by holding on to the rear of the swiftly moving carriage, he might get a lick of the whip.

The guiding principle of most managements in India was to show the workmen who was boss, to keep the men in "their places". "Show the least sign of weakness," they said, "and you're lost."

Sir Dorab Tata, at the general meeting of the shareholders that year and the year before, had predicted the changes which would take place, and advocated keeping ahead of them by more attention to labour welfare and to adjustments in wages. And, after the strikes of 1920, most India managements did try to adjust themselves to the new era, although many of them saw its outlines only dimly. Management needed contented workmen. Labour welfare in living conditions in the town and in working conditions at the plant came to take, or at least to share, first place.

A safety-first movement was inaugurated at Tata's in that same year, under a general committee implemented by departmental sub-committees. Foremen vied with one another to reduce accident percentages in their departments. Posters displayed in all offices and mills sought to make everybody safety-minded. K. A. D. Naoroji, the grandson of Dadabhai Naoroji, who was the first Indian to sit in the House of Parliament, took on the bulk of the promotion work. He set aside one period each year as safety and health week. Prizes were awarded for hundreds of original posters and sculptured models shown during that week.

A woman had been run over by a locomotive at a grade crossing near the blast furnaces. One young Indian artist built a miniature furnace in exact scale, ran a tiny railroad track in its proper place, made a diminutive locomotive and iron ladles. Under the wheels of the engine he placed a small human body, smeared with red paint. Deaths from crossing railroad tracks carelessly almost ceased in a short time.

Heretofore, many workmen had avoided the company's hospitals and first-aid stations. They felt that a poultice of cow dung applied to the forehead would relieve fever more quickly than a dose of quinine given free at a company hospital. Even during an epidemic of smallpox it was hard to get the workmen to a dispensary for inoculation. Nowadays, if there is a widespread infection, the company inoculates the townspeople at the rate of 10,000 a week.

Eventually the company installed an X-ray theatre in their hospital, but many of the men were as superstitious about its workings as westerners are apt to be about sitting down thirteen at a table. "Only a devil could look through a person's body," they said, and recalled two instances which proved X-ray to be the functioning of an unnatural agent. One was of the thief who was arrested after he had stolen a necklace and some rings. The jewellery was nowhere to be found in his room or his clothes. The man became ill, but refused any medicine. The X-ray revealed the missing baubles cached in his stomach. Surely it was the deed of a devil to see *inside* a man's innards.

Then there was the workman who acquired a limp as a result of an accident. He came back from his native village with a letter from his doctor stating that the man had suffered a bad fracture. He was given a watchman's job in which he could sit down all day and still draw his pay. Finally he was persuaded to have an X-ray. The plate showed that he had never had a fracture or other bone injury. But he wasn't told just then. As he limped away from the hospital, somebody yelled at the top of his lungs, "Look out!" And the man sprinted a good hundred yards in fine style.

Over the years, however, the Indians have become entirely accustomed to the X-ray machine and no longer have a superstitious fear of it. For one thing they have handled it themselves in analyzing large ingots, which are X-rayed before being forged into shafts for ships, as are large castings or forgings which are to be finished into heavy-duty products. The operators may be graduates of American or European universities; they are certain to be Indians.

With the inauguration of the safety-first movement, suggestion boxes were placed in all departments. Ninety per cent of the letters contributed by the workmen had nothing to do with the welfare of the men in general. Some were simply leg-pulling, some were just naive, but they were all interesting.

One letter requested the management to remove a very troublesome woman from a specified neighbourhood. She was said to be incorrigible and the owner of a vile tongue. Unfortunately, the writer continued, no man could withstand her blandishments. If the management doubted this, it was suggested that the general manager send for the woman and observe what effects she had on him !

Another letter suggested that the works be shut down during the hot months of April and May. The men could enjoy themselves in their native villages, especially if the company paid their railway fare and continued their salaries. Then the men would produce far more steel during the cooler months.

A learned Brahmin asked that the company add a department to the plant. Iron had been used in ancient times as a medicine, he wrote. Why not produce medicinal iron now?

One man showed his imagination by suggesting that the blast furnaces be tapped through a long pipe shaped like a rail. One would then have only to water-cool the templet and would immediately have railroad rails without the expense of great rolling mills for shaping steel ingots. Another proposed that women employees be given three months' leave before, and four months' after, confinement, with graduating bonuses for large families. Soon, he continued, it would be unnecessary to bring men from distant points in India, for these subsidized generations would be steel-minded from the cradle.

One suggestion was later considered seriously. It was to build a canal from the collieries to Jamshedpur, some eighty miles. The ancestors of this man had worked for centuries on the Hooghly River barges.

The installation of a trolley-car system inside the plant was advocated to connect at the various gates with branches which would transport the men who lived in distant suburbs. Also the piping of filtered water to all departments, in place of the free carbonated water which was then furnished. Charged water, the writer claimed, gave him indigestion. As a matter of fact, one can now drink cool filtered water anywhere in the plant.

An employee in the brick department wanted the company to compel women workers to wear brassieres. He found it difficult, he said, to keep his mind on his job when women brought bricks for him to lay. He attributed this to the fact that he was temperamentally unstated to work in amorous surroundings.

An Indian Christian suggested that his sect should receive higher wages because they dressed in shirts, pants, and shoes, while the other Indians still wore loin-cloths and *dhoties*. "Our garments cost more," he pointed out to the manager. "Since you are also a follower of the illustrious prophet Mr. J. H. Christ, Esq., you will please take the necessary steps."

The committee which judged these letters awarded cash prizes for approved suggestions, many of which were of actual value in scientific improvements for both accident reduction and higher operation efficiency. No trolley cars run through the plant today, but highways for cars and buses connect all departments. Millions of dollars have been spent on projects which grew out of the ideas of illiterate Indian workers on the sand-beds.

There are very few illiterates working at Tata's nowadays and no more sand-beds. Blast furnaces no longer require sand-beds. Any iron produced above steel-furnace requirements now is cast over pig machines. Some people say that iron poured over machines is inferior for foundry purposes to sand-cast iron; it is, however, undoubtedly better for steel-making.

I have often heard references to the "dumb" millions of India. They are dumb in the sense that they are not represented in their Government; but the word as it is frequently employed by Anglo-Saxons is a synonym for "stupid", and they are stupid because they don't speak English. I am always reminded of the old fellow who worked in the rolling-mills, Bob, from Cumberland. Once a month Bob would come to my bungalow with four plain cardboard slips. I would write the address of his family on one side and on the other some phrase like "Bob in the pink". Each week Bob would put a stamp on one and mail it. He couldn't write, and the weekly card covered his correspondence. Yet Bob was deeply contemptuous of the Indian workmen and what he called their "ignorance". As he drained his whisky-soda, he would say, "We'll never be able to teach them dumb fellows how to roll steel. They know no't abaht our language, and I don't bloody well want to waste ma time learnin' them beggars how to talk."

Yet I have known few Indians who were not reasonable, intelligent, and—when they were not apathetic from malnutrition—eager to learn. They are in extreme contrast to their warlike neighbours on the north-west, the Afghans. Not many Afghans are anything like my highly spiritual Hindi teacher, Abdulla Rahman Khan. As a people they are fierce fighters and fierce haters. I knew another Afghan worker at Tata's, a man who came back to work some weeks after he had been terribly beaten and maimed. He was a fine fellow and a good friend. I asked him if he knew who had beaten him. He said yes.

"Why don't you report it to the police?" I asked.

He smiled. "The days are long and many," he replied. "I can wait and hate."

Some months later the headless body of a man was found on a dump, burned by the molten slag. The body was never identified, but his colour and what was left of his clothing showed that the man had been an Afghan. I noticed that my Afghan friend was thenceforth in the best of spirits. He told me he had never felt better. I looked at his crooked leg and then at his face. He was silent, but his eyes radiated happiness. As I turned to leave him, he murmured, *"Jo hoga, so hoga"*—"What will be, will be." He lived to enjoy his revenge for some years. Then somebody stuck a knife into his guts and turned it around a dozen times, as you would a corkscrew. His body was also mutilated.

Afghanistan has been a source of worry to England for a century. A large force of English soldiers was permanently stationed on the border. Incredibly enough, the British Government actually paid a yearly tribute of about $700,000 to the tribal chiefs of Afghanistan to guarantee peaceful relations. The nominal purpose of the payment was to indemnify the Afghans for the tolls they had formerly levied on caravans passing through, but it kept them quiet. England has always had respect for the small mountainous country. It is a bad man's land. Kipling tells what the women there have done to wounded British soldiers and warns the Tommy to save his last bullet for himself:

When you're wounded and left on Afghanistan's plains,
And the women come out to cut up the remains,

Just roll to your rifle and blow out your brains—
And go to your God like a soldier.

Some British politicians say Afghanistan is not worth annexing to India, since its produce and raw materials would not fatten the British purse. Others argue that it is better to keep it a sovereign state to act as a buffer between India and Russia. When Lord Curzon visited Afghanistan fifty years ago, the Amir twitted him about the lawlessness in England. In Afghanistan, he said, only twenty-seven murders had been committed during a whole year. Those twenty-seven murderers had been brought to trial and each had received the sentence, "Let him never be seen by anyone any more".

That same Amir came to Bombay in the course of a visit to India. British officials took him on a tour of the harbour, where some warships were tied up, and all over one of them from stem to stern. They may have hoped to impress him with the might of the British Navy, but he was quite as impassive as if he saw great battle-wagons every day. On leaving the ship, however, he noticed and remarked on the guard of soldiers on duty at the quay. He was told the soldiers were there to keep unauthorized people from going on board.

"Would it not be simpler to put up a sign warning people not to go near the ship?" he asked. The escorting officers said they didn't think a mere written notice would be effective.

The Amir laughed. "India must be a queer country," he said, and went on to tell his companions that to protect his beautiful new gardens laid out near Kabul he had posted a sign reading, "No trespassing, by order of the Amir". Two men, however, had disobeyed the injunction. He had been asked what punishment they should receive. He had answered, "Make sure that they never again walk in the garden". Perhaps, he added thoughtfully, his Minister had taken the order a trifle too literally. The legs of both men had been cut off above the knee. The example had restrained any other prospective strollers.

Gin Bill and I once heard another story about the Amir from an American dentist who had lived in the royal palace for a month. The Amir was bothered by a couple of teeth, and a dozen or so of his wives were complaining of toothache. The Amir was progressive, so he sent to Calcutta for the American dentist, providing also a considerable sum of money for travelling expenses. When the dentist arrived at the frontier he was met by a guard of fifty soldiers, all of them over six feet. With his escort he proceeded to Kabul on horseback.

At the palace, the dentist placed the Amir in a chair and took a look at the offending teeth. They were ulcerated and the entire mouth was in bad shape. He explained the necessity for an extraction, promising that he would give him gas to make his patient oblivious to pain. The Amir looked anxious. He asked how long the unconsciousness would last. The doctor said it would be several minutes. No, the Amir replied, he could not afford to be unconscious for a single minute in his kingdom, except in his well-guarded bedroom. The job had to be done without anaesthetic. When the doctor told him he could not stand the excruciating pain without gas, the Amir laughed and calling in one of his Ministers, said, "Remove two similarly placed teeth from his mouth without an anaesthetic. I will see how he takes it."

The doctor didn't dare disobey. He knew the Amir's reputation. Unfortunately the Minister had a perfect set of teeth. The dentist gripped a molar with his forceps and yanked it out. The victim yelled and carried on as though he were being murdered. The Amir remarked that one tooth would be enough, another extraction might kill the man or drive him to insanity. He detailed two guards to hold the Minister, who was still moaning, while the dentist went ahead with his own extractions. And although the ulcerated teeth must have been infinitely more painful to lose, he made no sign except one slight wince.

When it was over, the Amir jumped from the chair, drew himself up, looked at the agonized Minister, and smiled. Turning to the dentist, he said, "Dogs and kings are different, aren't they?"

Nor was that the end of the story. After fixing up some eighty ladies of the harem, and learning to play parchesi with the Amir, the dentist left, receiving no less than 10,000 rupees for his work. The money was placed in his saddle-bag and another guard of fifty soldiers galloped up to take him to the frontier. The doctor began to worry. What if he were robbed and then murdered in the mountain fastnesses of Afghanistan?

The Amir guessed the doctor's thoughts. He smiled and said, "I have also considered such a possibility. I have arrested and imprisoned the wives, mothers, sons, and daughters of the guards. If you lose a single rupee I shall kill all the hostages. So if even one guard attempts to steal even one rupee, there will be forty-nine guards to prevent him from doing it."

I have never been in Afghanistan, but I am living in hope of doing so. Among the hundreds of Afghans who have worked for me, some have been very dear friends. They are fine workers at a job where they can see the tangible results of their labour and are quite useless for ordinary work. If you give them a destructive job and make them do it in an orderly way, they will soon get tired and quit. Tell them to demolish the Empire State Building, commencing at the top and lowering stone, brick, and steel safely and they would be absolutely no good at it. But tell them simply that you want that building out of the way within a week and they will work twenty-four hours a day. They would, however, do it in their own way. With hydraulic jacks and dynamite they would calmly topple the building over into the street. If it crashed into other buildings in falling, they would look on and hold their sides in laughter; in fact, the more buildings destroyed the happier the workers.

I have seen a crowd of Afghans level a large open-hearth furnace to the ground in a couple of days. They spoiled a hydraulic jack, they broke cables on a 150-ton overhead crane; they cooled red-hot holes a little with water and then fired them with dynamite. And they had the time of their lives. They must always produce results immediately or lose interest. But they are great soldiers and not without honour. They remind me of Xenophon's summing up of the character of Gyrus after the battle of Cunaxa. It might be said in paraphrase that, "To whom an Afghan is a friend, he is a good friend. To whom he is an a enemy, he is a bitter enemy."

Most of the Indians I have worked with showed a sharply contrasted persistence. One of the best blast-furnace men in India while still in training was ordered by his foreman to act as cinder-snapper for a time. The cinder-snapper opens the slag-notch, lets the slag run off, and then bots up the water-cooled notch with an iron bot. This Indian boy was trying hard, but he couldn't bot up the notch, commonly called a monkey, very well. He got flustered. An old Indian cast-house man walked over and stopped the notch with ease. He had had years of practice. The young student was filled with rage and despair. Tears ran down his cheeks. He shouted at me, "God damn it! I'll never be a blast-furnace man. I'm just no good."

I patted him on the back. I confessed that after years of trying to be an expert at that job I was not yet very proficient. He calmed down and answered that he was going to learn to do that job or go to hell trying.

If that quality of determination were not present in most Indians, it might not have been feasible to effect the gradual Indianization of Tata's. During the first World War the company's directors had not thought much about training Indians to take the place of imported nationals of other countries. But during its course many of them went to Japan on business; they met Japanese steel-men and saw how their plants were run. The mills were operated entirely by Japanese, although Americans had been used to establish the industry and get it running. Returning to India, the directors recalled that when the original small steel plant came into operation Tata's had employed only two Europeans in the boiler-plant and power-house, and only two in the electrical department, the chief engineer and his assistant. All the operators were Indians and dozens of those under the chief engineer held university degrees.

No non-Indians had then, nor have they since, sat on the Tata board of directors. The participating directors of the agents' firm, Tata and Sons, have all been Indians, although occasionally foreigners have acted for a time as special paid directors, or advisors.

The Tatas had always intended that the company should be entirely Indian. After the various directors had returned from their very instructive trips to Japan there was a general agreement that the Indianization of the company was not only desirable but altogether possible as soon as the war should be won. The directors had before their eyes many concrete examples of Indian ability.

The electrical department of a steel plant is its nerve centre, upon which efficiency and production capacity both depend. In 1915 an able Bengali electrical engineer, S. Chose, had succeeded the European chief engineer. From then on, in fact until 1926, the electrical department was run altogether by Indians.

The coke-ovens operated for the first years under a Princeton graduate, Jay Slee, and three Welsh general foremen, but the rest of the coke-oven men were Indians. Then another Bengali, D. C. Gupta, a husky young Harvard Bachelor of Science who had been third furnace hand in the open-hearth steel department, was insulted by a big Yorkshire foreman. Gupta said calmly to the man that he had been too long in America to take reflections on his parentage without a fight. The foreman made a pass at him. He dodged and landed a haymaker on the foreman's jaw, putting him out for the count.

Consternation swept the town. An Indian had challenged a British foreman to a fight and knocked him out—an Indian had struck a Britisher.

Old Tutwiler raised hell with Gupta—at least he went through the motions—wearing his most intimidating expression. Secretly he was pleased with the young Indian who had so much guts. Gupta went to work in the coke-oven department, where with his knowledge of chemistry it took him only two years to become superintendent, Not long after, when the Welsh foremen were replaced by natives, another highly technical department was thereby completely Indianized. Gupta was only one of the millions of "dumb" Indians, but his success was not an accident. After eight years' service as superintendent, during which time three new batteries of Wilputte by-product coke-ovens were built, Gupta resigned to become Director of Industries for Bihar and Orissa, and was largely responsible for the industrialization of that province.

A. C. Bose, another young Bengali and a graduate of Carnegie Tech, joined Tata's as a chemical engineer and worked up to the post of chief chemist, replacing an American. Since then none but Indians have been employed in the company's laboratories.

In 1919 Sir Dorab Tata, reviewing what these young Indians had accomplished, pointed out to the company directors that if Indians could be educated and trained abroad to take over from foreigners highly technical jobs successfully, they could also be educated and trained at home. He proposed an Institute of Metallurgical Technology in Jamshedpur. The directors were so enthusiastic that within a year a large building with laboratories, lecture halls, classrooms, and a library was built and equipped. Three excellent Britishers and a number of ranking Indian instructors formed the nucleus of the teaching staff. The students were to receive enough pay for each month to cover living and incidental expenses. We advertised for students, stipulating that they must be Bachelors of Science from accredited Indian or foreign universities, and offering rail and travelling costs to the men we wanted to interview.

Out of the 1,000 applications which poured in on us, we selected 200 from which to pick the final twenty students we could enrol in the school. Out of that first group of twenty, one is now superintendent of open-hearth furnaces, one is superintendent of the duplex plant, a third is superintendent of the order department controlling the rolling programme, a fourth is head of the Institute itself.

We were careful to select men whose physical endowment would fit them for three years of stiff training, the first of which was a vigorous course in steel-mill metallurgy with constant observation trips to the plant. We allowed enough time for and encouraged participation in all sorts of sports. The second year called for alternate periods of study at the Institute and work in the various plant departments. The students were not then observers but actual labourers at the command of their foremen for any kind of work. By the end of the second year the students have a pretty good idea of which department they prefer, and the foremen have been able to form an opinion of the human material available. Then by agreement between students and superintendents each boy is assigned; he is expected to devote all his time to an intensive study of his chosen department. If he has picked, for instance, the blast-furnace section, he must read all the technical literature ever published in England, Germany, France, and the United States, so that he becomes a sort of walking encyclopaedia on blast furnaces. When his superintendent first begins to fire questions at him, he is expected to look up the answers, but not for long. In everyday practice a man has to be able to do the right thing instantly, without stopping to figure it out. By the time he has a second thought in an emergency, he may be too dead to need it.

I can remember a night in Gary, Indiana, when I was casting old No. 9 furnace. It was ten below zero. I was leaning against a column when the furnace slipped and burned the blow-pipe directly behind me. White-hot coke came flying out like buck-shot from a gun. I decided to run for it. I pulled up the collar of my mackinaw and started straight down the cast-house as fast as I could go under a barrage of burning coke. Just as I thought I couldn't make it, the wind was slammed off the furnace with a roar and the air was no longer filled with coke missiles. Back at the furnace I found my general foreman, Jim Gouger, who had come along just in time to see what had happened, take it in, and without hesitation fall on the lever controlling the cold blast valve and so shut off the blast. He had acted instinctively. Jim grinned at me.

"This is a hell of a day to pick to go out, man," he said. "Don't you know it's pay-day?"

As the Institute continued to turn out top-flight technicians over the years, the European department heads became uneasy. All graduates entered company service at fairly high salaries. The Europeans claimed that their labour costs were rising because of these salaries. Actually they feared for their jobs. Many of them had little or no higher education. They had learned what they knew by doing it. They could see the day coming when graduate students would replace them.

Many young men who were refused entrance to the Institute went to England, Germany, and the United States to secure their Master's degrees, feeling sure that when they came back Tata's would give them suitable jobs. Soon we were inundated with applications from such graduates. The fathers of boys who were turned down because they were physically unfit often went to friends in the legislature and started campaigns against the company. They even charged a sort of nepotism, saying that Parsi boys were favoured over the others, which was not in the least true.

There were some cases in which Tata's took in one or another promising young man against their own better judgment. A brilliant young Bengali, conceded to be among the best mathematicians in India, had been refused first because he looked ill, and second because he was twenty-five, and therefore over the age limit. After he gained his degree in Germany and spent two years in coke plants, benzol and sulphuric installations, he returned to India. We gave him a highly paid post in coke-oven and coal-research work. A few months later he began coughing blood and having to stay home from work. A short time later he was dead.

Twelve years after the Institute opened, we made some radical changes. We had had an apprentice scheme of sorts for the sons of illiterate old employees, my own pet project. We decided to tie this in with the Institute and at the same time to raise Institute standards by inviting men to join who had still higher qualifications than the men then on the teaching staff. To add, in other words, a branch somewhat like post-graduate seminars in American universities, where men could train for the top jobs.

Up until this time the Institute had accepted sizable yearly grants from many provincial Governments. The Institute heads, though, were bound in return to take in a certain number of students each year from the donor provinces. The advantage in this arrangement was that it made the Institute cosmopolitan. But it also tied the hands of the entrance board in the selection of candidates. Now the Institute refused any further grants. It was free to pick men solely on merit and physical stamina.

Graduates of Indian or foreign universities with their B.S. degrees were newly classified as B men, and the apprentices as C. Above both of these we instituted a higher grade with two divisions, A1 and A2, which provided only two years of training. The A1 students were drawn from university masters or doctors of science, but must also have actually worked abroad in the steel industry for two years. And they must pass a physical-fitness test. The A2 students had to have the same educational background, but were not required to have had practical working experience. A1 men received about $100 a month, and A2 around $70.

We had one employee without much formal training who did very well for himself on a foreign mission. He was a big, rangy fellow from the Bombay side, who had charge of the rail and structural finishing department, where rails are straightened and structural sections are cut to required length. We bought a large rail-straightening machine on the Continent and decided to send this foreman to Germany to observe the assembly of the costly and intricate machinery, and to have a look, too, at Continental finishing methods.

When he came back he described the royal manner in which he had been treated, particularly after he had had some business cards made. The Germans he met all had large cards with strings of initials after their names. He showed us one of his own cards, a huge affair with fluted edges. After his name appeared the letters F.B.A.B.U. This evidence of erudition impressed the Germans tremendously, and no one was so rude or so anxious to display his ignorance as to ask what the letters stood for. I asked him, however. With a twinkle in his eye he replied, "They stand for 'Failed in Bachelor of Arts, Bombay University'".

One of the prime movers in the establishment of the Institute was a young Indian by the name of Prem Mathur, who had learned the open-hearth game the hard way. He had worked his way over to America on a boat and had taken any job he could get to earn enough for schooling. After finishing at the Ford apprentice school Prem went into Ford's open-hearth department, putting aside any observance of his caste and performing the most menial tasks while he worked his way up. Back home, Mathur got himself made chairman of the Institute committee, where he could exert all possible pressure to keep the school going and expanding. By 1928 he was assistant superintendent of the Tata open-hearth department.

The Institute has proved its value many times over, in many ways. Tonnage figures reflect also improvements in other respects. Still they are significant. In January, 1919, the open-hearth department went all out for record production, with all seven furnaces in top condition. The weather was cold and rather wide war-time specifications still held. Americans and Britishers manned the furnaces, and most of their first and second hands were Anglo-Saxon. Everything broke right. They hung up a record of 19,200 tons of ingots that month, a record for all time, since stricter specifications were about to go into effect. When the tonnage was announced, the Blood Tub was the scene of a super-celebration which set its own kind of record.

In 1923, when the first Institute graduates were working in the plant, we had a plentitude of heavy melting scrap from the duplex plant, and better furnace design and better gas producers. The monthly tonnage then averaged around 23,000 tons. By 1928, when the Institute graduates had worked up to responsible jobs, three of them actually operating furnaces, the open-hearth department turned out an average of 28,600 tons of steel ingots.

By 1932 the American depression of 1929 began to hit India with full force. It was no longer necessary to run seven furnaces in the open hearth; the duplex furnaces alone could, in fact, have carried the load for ingots. We decided that if ever there was a time to try out the Institute boys to the limit, this was it. We transferred a few Americans and Europeans to the duplex plant and sent the rest home. I handed over the open hearths to Prem Mathur and his trained men, telling them the department was their baby; they had to run it or quit. There was a lot of criticism of this move. Even some Indians were sceptical. A few people actually suspected me of trying to show the Indians up, to prove that Europeans and Americans were still really needed there!

After a little initial nervousness, the Institute boys settled down, and when times improved a bit they were ordered to run on full production. Within a year they were averaging 34,000 tons a month and had set a record for one month of 37,000 tons, or nearly double the American and British Tata record of 1919.

Now the duplex steel plant is operated by Indians with an Institute man as superintendent, and only a couple of Europeans retained more or less as pensioners. The production runs around

700,000 tons of ingots a year. And the rolling-mills are operated entirely by Indian labour under Indian supervision.

I doubt very much if Tata's could ever have achieved the Indianization of the technical personnel of the plant without the Institute. That they have done so is cause for gratitude not only from the sons of India but from the entire British Commonwealth of Nations. Within the country, the Institute soon commanded an attitude of respect and admiration. One Maharaja travelled 1,000 miles to go over the school and ask advice for his sons. Every time I hear Indian princes characterized as "medieval" I remember that man.

When he was shown into my office for a consultation, two of his sons were about to embark on careers. The eldest was already in a special Indian college being trained to rule in his father's place. The Maharaja wanted to send the second son to an American university for a degree in industrial engineering so that he could come back and supervise the production of lac in his father's State. The third son hadn't the necessary qualifications for the Institute. But since there were fine iron and manganese deposits in the principality, the Maharaja wished him to learn mining engineering and steel-mill practice, eventually to develop these properties. I was asked to recommend the best universities in the States for these two boys.

But important as it is, the Institute is only part of the whole giant Tata project. I have sat in the Institute grounds watching a tennis match between a technical student and the Kumar Sahib of Seraikela, heir to the throne of that State, and remembered the days when Jamshedpur was nothing but a few houses and a lot of thatched huts. And later days when the survival of the company itself hung precariously on the balance wheel of chance. Now, when green lawns and miles of comfortable dwellings, hundreds of acres of master steel plant and its satellite shops and mills, make the town one of the great prides of India and the envy of the covetous Japanese, it is difficult to realize that only thirty-odd years ago this same site was the undisputed hunting ground of leopards and tigers.

CHAPTER VIII

AN ELEPHANT FIGHT AND A WEDDING

I NEVER CARED much for the traditional sport of India, big-game hunting. As far as I can remember I went hunting only once, and that was when I was a newcomer in the country. Three of us, all recent arrivals, started out after a bear that had been raiding a village near by. I was armed with a .22-calibre rifle, one of the other mighty hunters carried a shotgun, the third had a .32-calibre revolver. Fortunately we never saw the bear. He might have given us a good spanking.

There is, however, plenty of big game in India for any sportsman's gun. I am reminded of a well-deserved rebuke administered to me by Jim Scott, the English commissioner in Chaibasa, who had settled the tin-plate workers' strike. An American shipboard acquaintance had asked me some time before what the chances were of bagging a tiger if he should come out to India. I had made large and alluring promises to arrange a shoot for him. When suddenly he arrived in Jamshedpur to collect his tiger, I wrote to Jim Scott, who was a well-known and successful hunter, suggesting that it would be to the advantage and pleasure of both men to go on a shoot together.

His reply, in part, read as follows: "If you think, Jack, that I am going to close my court and stop the wheels of government under my jurisdiction simply to take over the charge of some American, just because he does or does not happen to be a near-millionaire or what-not, and strike out through the jungle on a mad hunt for a tiger, you are very much mistaken. I have always given you credit for knowing that the first rule of hunting is to bring the hunter into close juxtaposition with the hunted. This requires time, patience and desire. At present I happen to possess none of these attributes."

I felt like a little boy who has asked the teacher for an afternoon off to go to a baseball game. As it happened, my American friend and the Commissioner subsequently met, became good friends and enjoyed not one but two shoots together on elephant-back. But that ironic remark that one must "bring the hunter into close juxtaposition with the hunted" is only too true. A few years ago, when an Englishman of exalted title visited the State of an equally exalted Maharaja, his host overlooked no detail to ensure a successful hunt. After the hunting party were safely ensconced in a *machan,* or blind, high up in a tree, thousands of beaters forming a large circle began moving forward, driving every sort of wild animal towards the centre where the *machan* was. But the thoughtful Maharaja, knowing quite well that there might happen to be no tigers in the neighbourhood that day, had arranged to have two of them "planted" there. The two most dispensable ones were taken from his private zoo and given a good shot of dope before being released well within the circle of beaters.

The host even arranged to have his best *shikari,* or hunter, beside the English lord in the *machan.* When the first tiger hove into sight, the Englishman fired at close range, perhaps a fraction of a second before the *shikari*. The animal dropped in his tracks. The second tiger ambled up. Again two shots rang out. Tiger No. 2 also dropped dead.

When the carcass of the first tiger was examined, the Englishman noticed that one bullet had passed through a hind leg, causing a mere flesh wound. The other had pierced the heart. The *shikari* apologized for his poor shot, insisting that it was the Englishman's marksmanship which had killed the tiger. The second tiger had also been struck by both bullets, but there was no occasion for apologies, since the shots had landed only inches apart. The hunt continued through the following day. A third tiger obligingly appeared, one which had never suffered the indignity of a zoo. The *shikari* withheld his fire. The Englishman dropped the animal with one shot.

Years ago I used to meet a fine old gentleman every time I went to London, very correct in his Savile Row tailoring, and looking not at all like a mighty hunter. But he had sixty tigers and much other game to his credit. A friend of mine shot deer with him in Orissa several times. One day, on reaching the top of a hill, they came upon a hundred or so fine black buck grazing just over the crest. The older man raised his gun and took aim. After a few seconds he lowered it again and said, "It would be criminal for me to shoot one of them. I couldn't possibly miss one or two."

For years the old gentleman shot from a *machan,* where even if he missed his shot he would still be safe from the tiger. When he had run up a score of eleven or twelve, he became disgusted with himself. He never shot again from a *machan*. Instead he always sat in a shallow trench dug in the ground near the kill with two single-barrelled express rifles. If he had missed with the first shot, he still had the second gun to bring down the charging animal. If he had missed with the second shot, well, that would have meant death, and no more than he felt he deserved.

The same mild-mannered old man used to tell a story of a young American who had come out to Calcutta with one ambition: to kill a tiger. He went to the Sundarbans, a low, malaria-infested district between the many mouths of the Ganges River. The youngster shot a tiger all right, but didn't kill him. The wounded animal crawled off into the deep grass. Our young cub left his *machan* and stalked his prey, breaking the cardinal rule of hunting.

Pushing through the grass, which was some six feet high, the young American found his tiger squatting on his hindquarters. The tiger roared so that the thick moist air quivered, but he did not move. The young daredevil shot him through the mouth. Later he found that his first shot had paralyzed the back legs of the tiger. That was a bad shot, but a lucky one. Had it hit somewhere else in the body, the tiger would undoubtedly have enjoyed a nice American dinner.

Alfred, Lord Tennyson, told a good story on himself. He was sitting in a *machan* one day with a *shikari,* watching a goat tied to a tree not far off as bait for a tiger. The *shikari* pointed out a tiger approaching for a meal. Tennyson took aim and fired. He missed the tiger, but killed the goat. Tennyson said he felt like all kinds of a damned fool. Then the polite *shikari* said to him earnestly, "Sahib, you have rid my country of a plague. That was one of the worst man-eating goats in India!"

Not all sportsmen are necessarily sports. I knew one who bragged of being a mighty hunter as well as of reading the Bible for an hour every day. I don't know how much of biblical wisdom he absorbed, but he was an excellent shot. He went out after a tiger which had killed a child some ten miles from Jamshedpur. The man rode one horse and had a groom lead another to the scene of the kill. The extra horse was a thoroughbred which had won fourteen races for its owner. Now it was old, with creaky pastern joints. The man had it tied to a tree as tiger bait. We all felt it served him damned well right when he waited three whole days and no tiger turned up.

The biggest of all hunts in India is an annual affair. Few Europeans have seen it, although it is held every spring only a few miles from Jamshedpur. When ploughing time comes and the young Santalis hitch up their oxen to get the fields ready they want to be reasonably sure that no tiger will delay their return indefinitely. No one knows when the custom began, but ever since the oldest inhabitant can remember 100,000 or so men and women get together to hunt an area some sixty miles from east to west and twenty miles from north to south, timing the gathering to finish in a flourish with the vernal equinox.

They form a cordon around the area. With the kettledrums sounding a continuous din on all sides, they advance with bows land arrows loosely ready in their brown, muscular hands. All the wild animals in the circle are driven toward the centre, and brush fires in the bordering hills keep any prospective prey from escaping. Like long, coloured snakes, the fires burn for weeks after the hunt has culminated in a grand jamboree.

Some years the Santalis bag many hyenas, jackals, leopards, and perhaps a tiger. But few Santalis would bother to go on the hunt nowadays except for the attractions provided on the side—archery contests, old rituals, dancing, and plenty of liquor. Once they're filled with strong drink, many of the little fellows dance and dance, faster and faster, until they run amok.

Tribal dances to the hypnotic insistence of beating drums can do strange things to people. Many a time I have watched tall, white-robed Afghans perform their native "club" dance.

They start with the kettledrums calling out a slow, dignified tempo. The beat is quickened and the volume of sound swells. Each man in the circle strikes with his club the club of the man behind him, and then of the man in front of him. Constantly, insidiously, the tempo rises, and with it the dancers' movements become wilder, more abandoned, until dancer and drummer alike are lost to themselves in the wildest frenzy. The watching crowd catch the infection and throw themselves recklessly about, in and among the dancers with their swinging clubs. Many a man has his skull broken. Or a dagger may find its way to his heart.

But the Santalis, as far as I know, have a unique feature of group activity in their merry-go-round. Since the custom has a certain religious aspect, the Government officials pretend not to know about it. I have seen American women faint and white men turn sick at the sight. Only one man I know of had enough scientific detachment to be able to take motion pictures of a "ride".

The merry-go-round is a crude contraption, built of a fifteen-foot pole with a revolving cross-arm at the top. From one end of the cross-arm a long rope reaches nearly to the ground. Two long grappling-hooks are attached to the other end. A man, crazed with liquor, makes it known that he wants to ride the merry-go-round. His back is smeared with pitchblende. The grappling hooks are driven into his back beneath the shoulder-blades. Pulling on the rope, the maddened crowd raises him into the air and, running round in a circle on the ground, make him dance and gyrate hideously above their heads. When he is brought to earth again, his back is smeared with pitch once more. If the man lives, he is thenceforth a privileged character in his native village.

Not all the sights one sees in India are quite so grim. Two old ladies of our circle, both of whom looked like characters out of *Pride and Prejudice,* were returning from a picnic on Mount Dolma when they were stopped by an elephant. It was a wrinkled, venerable animal, standing on the dirt road under spreading branches of a shade tree and swaying from side to side, as elephants do to keep mosquitoes from biting them. No amount of horn-blowing by the driver had any effect. The elephant stood his ground. Finally the driver left the elderly women to deal with the old tusker and ran back up the hill to a forest officer's bungalow to get help.

The officer himself was there, and arrived on the scene with the panting driver behind him, not knowing what horrid mishap might have befallen the old girls. There they were, standing in the middle of the road close to the elephant, waving their parasols frantically in the air practically in his face. The forest officer described the elephant's expression as one of simple amazement. The elephant must have considered the proceedings beneath his dignity, for after only a few minutes of parasol waving, he calmly took himself off into a thicket.

Jack Leyshon, general manager of the Tin Plate Company of India, tells a story about two bull elephants fighting under a bright electric light. It sounds like a fake unless you know something of the background.

Near an old town called Galudih, some twelve miles from Jamshedpur, were huge piles of slag which contained copper. They were relics of an ancient copper mine, operated perhaps during the time when Megasthenes, the Greek, visited India in the third century before Christ. Those primitive miners either didn't try to extract all the copper from their ore or they were just wasteful. Anyway, there was enough copper left to warrant re-working the piles of gangue and reopening the old mining-pit. Not far from the hoist-house over the mine was a water-hole which overflowed during the rainy season. The people living near by were often startled from their sleep by the roar of tigers, the shrill yelp of jackals, or the trumpeting of elephants, as they came to drink. In hot weather, the water-hole dried up, and the smaller animals, recognizing the superior claims of two aged bull elephants, went elsewhere for their water. But slowly the level of the pool declined, and when the two elephants met at the muddy edge, they roared and trumpeted angrily at each other.

On the chance of seeing an elephant fight, the manager of the copper company had a wire run from the mine head to the water-hole, connected to a high-power light in a tree. Several Americans and Europeans drove over to Galudih and sat with the manager for hours every night in the hoist-house, from which they could see the water-hole clearly. But in the end only the mine manager and a few Indians could boast of having seen the battle.

At dusk on a hot and sultry night the two bulls came from opposite directions, reached the edge of the pool, stopped, and glared at each other. Whenever one attempted to drink, the other one immediately charged. There was a tense wait, both elephants trumpeting from time to time and watching one another with their small, wicked eyes. Then a silent pause. They began moving and swaying their bodies, taking tentative steps, feeling for position. Suddenly, at the same moment, they both charged. After what seemed to the watchers a very long time, the two massive bodies straining and pushing, one of the bulls succeeded in driving a tusk deep between the ribs of the other.

His opponent, mad with pain, wheeled, and in doing so broke off the tusk embedded in his side. The earth shook as he charged full upon the elephant which now had only one tusk to defend himself with. It was soon over. The wounded bull gored his enemy to a bloody, quivering death. Then he stumbled painfully away among the trees until, fully a mile away, he could go no farther, fell to his knees, and died.

The next morning a crowd from Jamshedpur drove over to see the two bulls. They had both swollen up to nearly twice their size—a fearful sight. A couple of Americans furnished the comic relief. Armed with .22-calibre rifles, they posed for their pictures, standing with one foot on an elephant's side. If their friends back in the States didn't notice that the rifles were .22's, the two men probably even now enjoy the reputation of being mighty hunters.

Fishing in India appeals to me more than hunting. I don't belong to the school of contemplative fishermen who like to rig a line and then take a nap. When I go fishing I want action and plenty of it. Many of India's tanks are well stocked with *rohu* and *merrick,* both of them game fish. Pound for pound, the *rohu* will give you as sporting a fight as any Columbia River salmon. The *merrick* fights just as hard, but not for as long. But whatever you catch, it is de luxe fishing.

You are invited to fish a tank in the neighbourhood and accept for the following Sunday. Your host has his men ground-bait certain spots, preferably beneath leafy shade trees, every morning until you arrive. You find a chair placed for you under a large umbrella. A man baits your hook for you, casts your line into a likely spot, and hands you the rod. All you have to do is wait for a bite and pull in the fish.

When a *rohu* takes the bait, he will run out forty or fifty yards, often breaking water as he springs and dives and tries to free himself. Sometimes a *rohu* will turn and run towards shore, ploughing up the muddy bottom as he comes. A large *rohu* must be played until he tires, otherwise he will break your line; unless, of course, you are not satisfied with a sporting line, tested to break at fifteen pounds. There are plenty of *masheer,* too—not unlike the Canadian muskallunge. But sport of all kinds waits there in India for the seeking: tiger, crocodile, wild geese; the snipe, ducks and pigeons for the hunter with patience, and—for the man who likes to sit down once in a while—fishing.

That sort of fishing, and hunting in the grand tradition, are a part of the old India. Living in the heart of the industrial section of the country, I have still been privileged to join from time to time in the more regal observances of life which can no longer be found outside India. And nowhere else could the two—the old and the new—intertwine and mingle as they do here.

I was a guest at a small dinner in Bombay for the Maharaja of Bikaner some time ago. The Maharaja was a cultivated, witty man who kept the general conversation sparkling. After dinner he took me over to a divan, saying he wanted some technical information. "As you know," he began, "I purchase quite a tonnage of rails from your firm every year for my State railways. I hear you have started making high-manganese rails, supposed to be far superior to ordinary carbon steel rails, and much more expensive. Will you tell me, do you ask more for them because they cost more to produce, or because you think the market will bear a higher price for a better product?"

I explained to His Highness that the high price was based on lower yield and the added cost of ferro-manganese. "For instance," I said, "we usually produce seventy-eight per cent of first-class rails from ingots, that is, ordinary quality rails. But we find it difficult to get more than seventy per cent when rolling manganese steel rails."

In his subsequent questions about steel production, the Maharaja of Bikanir showed that he knew the subject well, was informed in regard to quantity and quality of iron ore and coal in the country compared to American resources and production, and the aptitude of Indians in industry. This Maharaja was the man who in 1914 cabled to his King-Emperor George V and placed a million of cavalry and infantry at his disposal. He is the same man who made the same offer to George VI, adding that "after that one million, there are fourteen million more to follow".

My wife and I received an invitation to the wedding of the heir to the throne of Patiala to the daughter of the Maharaja of Seraikela. It came during the visit of a charming American widow from Youngstown, and we secured an invitation for her, too. She couldn't believe her eyes when it came. But there it was, a large oblong card with crest and coronet and letters in gold. She travelled to Seraikela with us and showed us a book she was reading by her favourite author, Louis Bromfield. It was fun to play the genie. When I told her that the very next day she would not only meet Louis, but sit at dinner with him, she was like a little girl before a Christmas tree. India already seemed like a magic land to her—make a wish and it was granted. To see a real Maharaja was enough—to meet Louis as well was almost too much.

The capital town of Seraikela and the palace of the Maharaja are not more than fifteen miles from Jamshedpur in a straight line across the Karkai River. There is no automobile bridge across the river, so one merely fords the river by boat, gets into a car, and half an hour later arrives at the palace.

It is much more pleasant to motor to Seraikela, however, because the road leads through some seventy-five miles of rural India in a circuitous route. It is like driving from the figure six on a clock all the way round to the left and arriving at the figure four. Once arrived at the Maharaja's guest-house, one can see quite clearly the sky-glow from the Bessemer converters in Jamshedpur.

In the sharp light from thousands of electric lights, we witnessed a strange and wonderful sight on that trip. Silhouetted against long lines of shining Cadillacs, Daimlers, and Rolls Royces paced two even longer lines of men in medieval dress, bearing blazing torches which leapt and danced in the night. In the centre of this avenue of flickering light rode the kinsmen of the groom, slowly one after another on elephant-back, and finally the Kumar Sahib himself, coming in state to claim his bride.

One had deliberately to put the anachronism of modern motor-cars out of mind, to see undisturbed the rich gleam of the trappings which fell straight to the softly thudding feet of the elephants, the gay dress and sparkling jewels displayed by both men and women, and—most magnificent of all—the bride daughter of the Raja Aditya Pratap Singh Deo of Seraikela whose ceremonial garments repeated the designs dictated to and hallowed for, her ancestors by their ancestors.

Our arrival in the palace grounds had had no accompaniment of pomp, but there was a certain etiquette to be observed. The women proceeded to the Maharanee's quarters to pay their respects. We men, among us the indefatigable Frank Estep went directly into the great hall, where a brilliant society was gathered.

Weaving in and out of the throng were dancing-girls, show girls and singers, story-tellers and conjurers, smiling and performing for whatever guests chose to heed them. Our party sat down on gilded chairs and watched, not without some awe that such fabulous entertainments existed and we were there to see them. It is no more than the bare truth that sometimes light reflected from some of the enormous jewels blinded us for are instant, like the rays of the setting sun on a distant window-pane.

The Maharaja of Patiala looked my way. I bowed. We had met at Poona and at Bombay. When he called me over I introduced Pop Estep. "Let us get out of this into an anteroom where we can have a talk and a drink," the Maharaja said.

We followed him. In a side room a bearer immediately appeared with a tray of drinks. The Maharaja's favourite nautch girl began silently to dance. He waved his hand in a signal of dismissal. Patiala was dressed in state with a large diamond, about the size of a pigeon's egg, forming the clasp which fastened the aigrettes to his turban. Long, pear-shaped pearls hung from his ears, and perfectly matched pearls encircled his neck and flowed down into his lap. The string of pearls I knew about. It was estimated to be worth two million sterling. I couldn't even guess the value of the diamond. It was strange to look at the picture of almost incredible Oriental opulence confronting me and remember the man as I had seen him standing on the cricket held, reckoned the greatest player of his day and, with Ranjitsinhji and Constantine, among the greatest players of all time.

We were not, however, discussing sports, but machinists, iron and steel, malaria, black-water-fever control. The Maharaja asked how many Sikh mechanics we employed and how they compared with American and British workmen. "We have about four thousand Sikhs in the various plants in Jamshedpur," I said, "and I consider them the equals of the British and Americans in every way."

He told us something of the land reclamation he was carrying out in his State, and of the benefits he hoped to bring his people with his many irrigation projects.

Later our own party rejoined forces and were taken on a tour of the gardens by Seraikela's son. The Bromfields arrived from a tiger shoot in the north with the Maharaja of Cooch Behar and their common friend, Haroun al-Raschid Beg. The young widow from Youngstown met several more resplendent Maharajas, but I could see that she was afraid she was dreaming and even more afraid she would wake up.

The wedding ceremony, entirely separate from the general festivities, was barred to us males, but not to our wives. The feminine guests were led through a door covered with vines into the garden reserved for the Ranee and the princesses. Near the centre ten or twelve steps led to a raised platform draped with soft rugs and tapestries. The steps themselves held rice, coconuts, incense, and oil tapers, each in its silver container ready for use during the wedding, in which, beside the bridal couple, only the priests and the ladies of the household took part. Their richly embroidered robes caught and reflected the subdued lights in a still lower key.

The women of our party stayed only an hour or so, for the intricate symbolism of the various and lengthy rites was obscure. The bride and groom were escorted here and there, on and off the platform, by their relatives and the priests, each movement accompanied by prayers, blessings, and the burning of oil and incense.

The garden was redolent with sweet-smelling shrubs and endless beds of fragrant annuals. Indian nights grow cool suddenly. Perhaps the young bride felt some slight touch of the chill through her heavy robes, at the gravity of the step she was taking. For neither the bride nor the groom had yet seen each other. The groom wore a shield on the side of his head which seemed to be fastened to his *pugree* and which hid that side of his face completely. The bride was never in a position to see the other side. We were glad we had seen them both, and knew them to be equally young and beautiful.

As we drove home through the first hint of dawn, we saw the Southern Cross over the deep Indian sky.

Seraikela, ruler of a State slightly smaller than Rhode Island which is inhabited by about one million people, is a hardworking man on ordinary days. During the hot season he usually presides at high court from six to ten in the morning; from ten until two in the afternoon he attends to affairs of state, consulting with his ministers about taxes, banking, loans, new dams, electrical installations, highways, the State chrome-ore and iron-ore properties. He takes, if he can, an hour's rest after tea, and goes back to his desk until seven. He seldom has time to go to Calcutta, but I have seen him there, in European tweeds and Bond Street linen. The Maharaja of Seraikela is the perfect example of the blending of the old and the new India.

I once read that Gray admitted taking fourteen years to complete writing the *Elegy*. There was a man in India whom we all knew, R. J. Campbell, who took fifteen years to gather material for one book and was paid so well that he could raise a large family at the same time. The subject of the book was the princes of India. Campbell, who was erudite, rather lazy, and a wonderful raconteur, would write a Raja and ask if he cared to have his family tree and his own history written up, if so Campbell would be glad to oblige for a consideration. Often he would live in the Raja's palace, dig into the old records, and when he had finished writing a number of pages at a fixed amount per page, he would be ready to move on to the next prince. Everything he wrote was, of course, censored. But he was so tactful that one Raja soon recommended him to another and our author was in great demand. Sometimes he spent months in a State, if the living was good and the wine plentiful enough.

As the ornate and ponderous tome which resulted was really published by subscription, few extra copies were made and there has never been another printing. Yet I should think that since the book was a comprehensive history of the period from 1890 to 1915, with a great deal of background material, it should be an interesting reference source. When I last saw the old man he was a clerk in a haberdashery and possessed only one, well-thumbed, copy of his single masterpiece.

Most of the palaces one sees in India, especially in Bengal, are owned not by Maharajas, nor even by the British, but by Armenians. After the battle of Plassey, in 1757, with which the infamous Clive established English rule in India, the British brought stability to Indian finances and government. In a short time a number of Armenians, attracted by that stability, went to India, and as a visible proof of the fortunes made there, built unbelievably beautiful palaces for themselves. The British were never interested in colonizing India, and only came out to amass riches or to earn pensions, returning to England when it was alone. They were content to rent their estates from the Armenians, who today own or control more real property in Calcutta than any other nationality. The Sassoons and the Davids, the Sassoon Davids and the David Sassoons, the Gaulstauns and the Ezras, and a score of others possess wealth beyond the dreams of man. They are the landlords of Calcutta.

Whenever an Armenian built a palace, he never neglected to duplicate the master mansion with a miniature in the rear, away from the servants' quarters. Nowadays these small dwellings are called coachman's or chauffeur's houses, but years ago they served their own purposes. They were referred to as *Bibi Khanas* and were happily occupied by the British Sahib's little Indian lady. The maternal ancestors of many Calcutta Anglo-Indians lived in such *khanas*, substituting for a Memsahib who refused to return to India, or acting as morganatic wife for a bachelor whose prestige forbade a legal tie.

The most amusing story I know about the resident of a *Bibi Khana* concerns the rather pompous wife of a Britisher who returned from England unexpectedly while her husband was in Simla. Walking in the garden the next morning, the woman noticed the "little lady" sitting in front of her tiny house. She went over and demanded to know who the little lady was and what she was doing there. With perfect courtesy, the dignified Indian replied, "I have been honoured, Memsahib, by acting in your place during your long absence".

Dignity, in fact, is a nearly unfailing Indian characteristic, I say "nearly" because in crowds Indians are excitable, too, and can quickly abandon the dignity they invariably show in a *tête-a-tête*. Once they are aroused, anything can happen. I saw a near-riot once, started by a pebble.

It was at a wrestling match on a Sunday afternoon in an unused rifle range which had been made into an arena. The mound of earth that had been a backstop for the targets had been terraced and turned into a grandstand. About ten thousand Indian wrestling fans were enjoying a very good exhibition. From time to time one of them who was seated on the mound would stand up in his excitement and obscure the view of those back of him. There would be shouts of "*Baitoe, baitoe*!"—"Sit down, sit down!" A youngster shouted at one such spectator, who paid no attention. The boy picked up a pebble and threw it at him. Abruptly the man stopped yelling encouragement at his favourite; he turned, infuriated, and, picking up a big piece of sod, hurled it through the crowd.

All at once everybody was reaching for something to throw. The air was thick with rocks. Suddenly the whole milling crowd started to surge down from the grandstands, close to panic. Some fifty policemen armed with long clubs were powerless to stop the onrush of men trying to get away. In five minutes the arena was empty except for about thirty men who had to be taken to the hospital. A tiny pebble had turned an orderly crowd of pleasure-seekers into a mob.

There were a number of Tata Indians in that crowd, and I was glad to see that they were among the few who kept their heads. Slim was one of them, the quiet boy who had sat around the sand-beds in the old days, listening while the others told their tall tales. Slim had just become a member of the first provincial Assembly of the Province of Bihar at the time of the riot, and had his position to consider. Nobody would have expected self-effacing Slim to progress from being a maker of pig-beds to labour leadership and subsequently to a seat in the Parliament.

Most of the men who used in the early days to enrich our story hour around the sand-beds were still with us a generation and more later: the giant, Gurumdin, the hashish smoker, Ali Baba, and Nally Wallah. Gurumdin had become a foreman and an excellent one, when I left India. In fact, the old man, spare and toothless, came down to the train to see me off. Ali Baba I had lost track of for many years after he had been transferred to the boiler-house. One day I was watching a tournament put on by the apprentice lads from the technical school, the Class C boys, who were employees' sons. One lad had excelled all the others in three events. When he came up to receive his prizes, an erect old man greeted him and then turned to me. It was Ali Baba. "This is my son, Sahib," he said proudly.

Nally Wallah, who had so loved to play the happy clown, had been at the same time a good worker. From the job of stove-tender, he was promoted to assistant foreman on a furnace. When, however, the Technical Institute commenced turning out highly skilled Indians for the plant, Nally Wallah dropped out of sight. Not unnaturally, he was resentful. "What if those boys have university degrees?" he said over and over. "Do they expect to know about blast furnaces in a few months of study what it took me twenty years to learn?"

From an amiable, conscientious worker, Nally Wallah turned into an embittered man who hung around with a bunch of hoodlums. Russian labour literature fired his ambition. He attended union meetings and became a labour leader. A group of his new pals, who were of the less desirable labour element, were arrested for burglary one spring, and he was sent to jail along with them. I talked the matter over with the magistrate; after serving eight months of his sentence, Nally Wallah was released. He came back to work, but as a stove-tender, under one of the highly trained Indians whom he despised. In later years he attained the vice-presidency of a union, but he was still only a stove-tender.

While one could understand why men like Nally Wallah were bitter and disgruntled, the high-caste Brahmin who is usually a clerk has more real reason for discontent. His standard of living is, of course, much higher than that of the average labourer, and his wage scale much lower. His education has been costly to himself and his parents. Part of the parental debt, at least, must be repaid. When he marries, he must live frugally and put aside marriage portions for his daughters. When the unions came into being, the high-caste Brahmin, permanently burdened with debt, sought relief by means of union support. But for several years the fact that he occupied executive positions in the Jamshedpur union, by reason of his schooling and training, was the very thing that weakened union power. The rank and file of the steel workers did not quite trust Madras and Bengal Brahmins to safeguard the interests of manual labourers.

And if the Brahmin and the rest of the class known rather loosely as *Babus*, or white-collar workers, were and still are badly off, the poor peasant farmer is at the bottom of the poverty scale. There is a great deal of misinformation disseminated about India and the Indians. But it is incontrovertible that some 5,000,000 Indians die every year from starvation. Many peasant farmers do manage to pay high taxes during lean years and still pull themselves and their families through, undernourished but still alive. Many do not.

About twenty years ago the district around Jamshedpur was on the verge of famine from lack of rain and the consequent failure of the rice crops. I was living then in a bungalow facing Beldih Lake, a small man-made tank of about five acres used to feed neighbouring paddy-fields. The lake had been stocked with fish. At noon one day we heard the muted babble of many voices. Outside, around the lake, we saw thousands of men and women, most of them pitiably emaciated. They formed a line along one end of the lake. The women pulled off their *saris*, pieces of cotton cloth a yard wide and about five yards long which are wound about their hips and draped over their shoulders, forming a dress. These they lowered into the water as a sort of seine.

Slowly, shoulder to shoulder, they advanced across the tank, driving the fish before them. When the first line had progressed some fifty feet, another line formed and followed them up so as to catch any fish escaping the front net. As we watched, the first line reached the shallows at the far side of the lake. Thousands of fish of all sizes leapt from the water and plunged desperately back again in vain attempts at escape.

The men, who had been standing up to their knees in water awaiting the moment to go into action, now waded out to the attack. They were armed with sticks, clubs, and empty Schlitz beer bottles. As a fish broke water, it was clubbed on the head with a beer bottle. That was the first time I had seen Schlitz bottles used for that purpose. The whole business lasted less than half an hour. By the time the police arrived, the starving tribe had departed, the richer by some thousands of fresh fish. But even this windfall could not last very long or extend to enough people, and there were a great number of deaths in the next few weeks.

Famines in India no longer reach the staggering proportions of generations ago. Improvements in agricultural methods, irrigation projects, extensions of the railways have helped. But only to a certain extent. The railroad mileage is impressive, but not nearly as great as it should be, considering the size of the country and the density of the population. Furthermore, while modern trains carry the passenger swiftly from one large town to another, they do not reach cross-country into the thousands of tiny hamlets which aggregate millions of souls. Commercially, there is no reason for them to do so, since traditionally the village has nothing to export to the city. And it requires little from the city that cannot be brought to it by bullock cart.

Whenever there is a rice shortage, such as the one that brought Bengal to the edge of famine early in the summer of 1942, it is a paradox that the wheat crop, which that year was a bumper one, does and can do very little to alleviate the general suffering. Even if the transportation system honeycombed every province, existing facilities, overburdened by carriage of troops and munitions, had been further depleted by the sending of a quantity of railway equipment to Iran to build the overland transport route to Russia.

Then, in spite of the fact that India grows one-eighth of the world crop, wheat is more generally used for food in the Punjab and the United Provinces than elsewhere. The other northern producing provinces have, ever since the Suez Canal opened the way to world markets, cultivated wheat mainly for export.

In addition, there is the curious quirk, common to human nature, which makes it difficult for the Indian villager, whose life and whose ancestors' lives have always been supported on rice or millet, to know what to do with a strange grain—when it can be got to him—even though he may be starving.

Many times I have actually seen large groups of peasants who were no more than skin-covered bones. Once a number of us, not knowing any better, gave such a group a quantity of cooked rice. After that one ravenous, desperate meal, most of the poor devils died. Their spleens had been inactive too long. I have seen nursing mothers with breasts as fiat as the pockets of a man's overcoat. I have watched whimpering, starving babies with just enough strength to grasp those barren breasts with their tiny, taloned hands and wring them in a vain effort to squeeze out a few drops of milk.

So stubborn, however, is the flickering vitality of the various racial strains which comprise the 390,000,000 people of India, that in spite of famines and droughts, and an annual death toll of 50,000 yearly from wild animals and poisonous snakes, the birth rate increases the population by 4,000,000 every year.

CHAPTER IX

BETWEEN THE DEVIL AND THE GERMANS

ONCE THE INDIAN Government had erected tariff barriers to protect the Indian steel industry, and the new Tariff Board was formed to promote the safeguarding of other existing and prospective Indian enterprises, we all expected Indian capital to once again flow freely. This didn't happen, however, and it isn't difficult to understand why.

The first protective tariffs were temporary. They could be lifted, if the Government should desire, before the young industries were full-grown. This policy was probably the result of pressure from British vested interests from without, and of fear on the part of a sincere enough group in India that the added duties would only further impoverish the Indian consumer while increasing the riches of the already rich shareholders of the companies affected. Strangely enough, the conviction was strong among the leaders of the *Swaraj*, or Home Rule, movement of the time, whose motto, "Support Indian industries, buy only Indian goods", did not keep them from being free-traders at heart.

A general lack of confidence in the future, and specifically an incredulity that the bureaucrats of the British Government could actually intend to foster Indian industries, paralyzed that normal release of fearfully withheld Indian capital. Such a state of affairs was most pleasing to the British capitalists, who seem without that regard for fair play which characterizes both the British people and the British Government. They promoted a much doubt and uncertainty as they could by the most insidious and effective bazaar propaganda. A year and a half after that duty on foreign steel was levied, Tata second preference accumulative shares were standing at twenty-eight on the Bombay exchange.

Even the American employees of Tata's lacked the confidence they should have had. The same D. M. Madan, the comptroller of accounts, who had tried vainly to persuade Tata employees into buying Tata Deferred back in 1913, had just returned from the United States, where he had been vastly impressed by the Steel Corporation and Bethlehem share sales plans for their workers. He proposed a pool of second preference shares for European and American employees to be bought in a block through Bombay financiers and the company and to be paid for in twenty-four monthly instalments. It took him months to put the project through. I later sold the block purchased then a ninety-four, and if I had held them until 1939 could have sold at 210.

Even had Indian capitalists been much stouter of heart, there was nothing in the labour situation to encourage them to loosen their purse-strings. The whole decade of the 1920's could hardly have been plagued with a more intense labour unrest, as lockouts, strikes, sitdown strikes and lightning strikes bedevilled employee and employer. The spare, ascetic figure of Mohandas Gandhi was no longer unknown to the diehard British industrialist.

An inconveniently literal adoption of Thoreau's philosophy of simplicity in living underlay Gandhi's doctrine of non-cooperation with the Government. Thoreau had once refused to pay his taxes in protest against some Government measure. Gandhi preached non-payment of taxes. The Government was a capitalist machine. If strikes hurt the capitalists, they also hurt the Government. Not necessarily formal, declared strikes—the new idea was the sitdown strike. Men would come to a plant prepared to work. Suddenly everybody would simply sit down for a few hours. The non-work period was called in Hindi a *hartal,* or halt. The union at Jamshedpur was still in disfavour with the men at that time, so the company could accomplish very little by negotiation. The only remedy seemed to be a lock-out. But lock-outs are costly.

One man, however, could always sway a mass meeting of workers with the power of his own simple and holy faith. I saw Mahatma Gandhi address some 60,000 persons in the grounds of the town hall. He was not expected until five o'clock, but the greater part of his audience were waiting patiently in their places by two. Just before five he arrived, with Motilal Nehru, C. F. Andrews, and half a dozen other prominent Indians.

When Gandhi mounted the platform and bowed to the people, a wild shout of welcome arose. "*Mahatma Gandhi ki jai!*" echoed against the distant hills. Here, I saw, was a great man. This frail framework of bone and muscle clothed in a few yards of homespun cloth had, through his love for his fellow men, attained the lonely grandeur of greatness. It seemed to me that this was no longer a labour meeting, but a convocation of men to hear the voice of one they believed holier than they.

Gandhi raised his hand to still the deafening acclamation. The gesture commanded complete silence. Then he began to speak, to exhort each man to give his utmost effort, in the knowledge that God would watch over him. Above all, he urged abstemiousness in all things, and complete faith in prayer. He spoke like a man inspired. I wondered what would happen in an American labour meeting if a union leader tried to persuade the men to depend on God, to offer prayers for better working conditions!

For a few years the management enjoyed a false sense of security. After all, there was a recognized union, and two or three high company officials were vice-presidents. Even if they held off from the local heads, the men seemed to like the president, C. F. Andrews—and we were turning out plenty of steel.

During this period the management changed. John C. Peterson, who was placed in charge in Bombay, and Charles A. Alexander, who became general manager, were both extremely progressive men. They had also, in 1925, the benefits of the pioneering work done by men like Charles Page Perin and T. W. Tutwiler, which was then bearing fruit. A lot of the credit for the present Tata plant belongs to the new men, but we old-timers who were there in the beginning remember what Old Tut and his boys did to keep the company alive and on its feet. They made mistakes, of course. But the mistakes were instructive, in point of fact, and as invaluable to the men who followed them as the accomplishments which everybody praised.

Peterson was the sort of man to give confidence to the local management in Jamshedpur. He O.K.'d any constructive proposal put to him without delay. To Peterson a man was right until he was proved wrong; if he was proved right he went up a step, if wrong, he dropped out of sight. I talked to him one night in 1927 on my veranda about furnace B. It needed a new lining. I told Peterson I thought the thing to do was to tear the whole furnace down and build a new one.

"How much will you make on a rebuilt B furnace," he asked, "and what would be the cost of a new furnace?"

"We will make 800 or 900 tons a day, which means we'd get iron for twenty-two rupees a ton, instead of twenty-eight as we do now,"

I said, pulling out the figures. "The new furnace would cost half a million dollars, and we'd need at least one new blowing turbine at $100,000. It would pay for itself in a year."

He thought a moment. "Go ahead and build your new furnace. I'll get the necessary sanction."

That was Peterson's way. Ordinarily such a proposal coming from the local head of an American plant would be subject to months of discussion at the main office.

I saw to it that the old pot was blown out and demolished before anybody had a chance to think up any objections. And by that time the engineering department had designs ready for a 22-foot hearth furnace. Despite a three months' strike which tied up labour, a brand-new B furnace took her place on the line only eleven months afterwards. And nine days after she was blown in she achieved the coveted 1000 tons a day.

I remembered then Charles Page Perin's advice to me to put in less time being a gentleman rider and more time getting a furnace that would do just that. I sent the old man a cable. I heard later that when he read the message, proud tears streaked his cheeks. I received a characteristic reply: "Congratulations stop we have grown up since we talked about a furnace producing 1000 tons a day stop what about a furnace that will produce a ton a minute?"

It wasn't long before D furnace, which had over 1,000,000 tons of pig-iron to her record, needed some attention. She had been a battler for the last two years, having broken through her hearth-jacket several times. Her column supports were burnt off, and reconditioning that old bitch was an engineering feat. With Perin's new challenge spurring my imagination, I tried to figure out a way of keeping the furnace in the air while we inserted new columns under her. The engineers said it couldn't be done. The whole furnace would have to come down.

But that man Perin had the power to stir men to more than their own known abilities. Why not, I thought, erect columns on a new base-ring just outside the present ones? Then put a new mantel-ring on top of the new columns? Then—build a new furnace shell into the old furnace a third of the way down from the top? That way the upper part of the furnace with all its equipment would be saved, and the existing skip-house would still be serviceable. Further, the new furnace would have a hearth diameter of 25 feet—why, it would be the largest furnace in the world !

Well, it was done. The new D furnace never made a ton a minute, but she did produce a record of 1392 tons in one day. And she's still standing.

With Perin in New York, Peterson in Bombay, and Alexander in Jamshedpur, we had a trio that really did things. It was an era for rounding off the rough edges of plant operation, for bringing the machinery of steel-making to a degree of perfection. A new spirit of achievement permeated the place. All department heads got to working co-operatively to bring their production to the peak.

Then a British railway official made a mistake. In 1927 the men in a great railway workshop struck for nearly two months. I learned the real story later, of the assurance given by the negotiating official to the strike leaders that the men would "lose nothing" if they went back to work. At the time, however, this was interpreted as a promise to pay some reimbursement. It was demanded and received. The men promptly called it strike pay. Labour in all the rest of India sat up and took notice. The strike fever spread. The unscrupulous among the labour leaders and agitators had a heyday. Illiterate workmen were called out to take a rest with the promise that the Government would force managements to accede to almost any demands.

Manech Homi was the son of an Indian engineer who had started out with the company in charge of the boiler and powerhouse under old Blaser. Manech began work on the open-hearth gas producers, was transferred to the by-product coke plant, and won a promotion to the traffic department. Both Manech and his father were ambitious, and the boy went off to Carnegie Tech for specialized training with two other lads, a young Parsi, Phiroze Kutar, and Jehangir Ghandy, who is now general manager of Tata's.

When Manech Homi came back he wanted, and was fitted for, a better job than the one he had left. But the management couldn't see it, and Manech turned to the law and to labour leadership. Then old Homi was fired by the management after many years of faithful service. Manech Homi conceived a deep hatred for the company which had, as he saw it, taken out on his father their prejudice against the son. He went on practising law, however, making at the same time an intensive study of labour-union structure, labour practices, and the statutes pertaining to labour. He realized that the strike which crippled an industry most while penalizing the worker least was the lightning strike, where only key men walked out and the other 90 per cent of the workers remained on the job, able to produce very little, but still drawing their pay.

In the middle of February 1928 the mills were running at top speed. Without warning one night all the drivers of the heavy-duty cranes failed to show up at ten o'clock for the late shift. The drivers of clean-up and other unimportant cranes were on the job as usual. We put some of them on to charging cranes. Instead of the regular hour and a half required to charge a furnace, these men took ten hours. We tried a green man to pour a heat of steel. He flooded the ingot moulds and boggies. The plant was effectively tied up without its key men.

The strikers referred the management to their lawyer and leader, Manech Homi. Homi had won the absolute confidence of every man in the plant. No management meetings were held. The men simple said, "Ask Mr. Homi. He is our leader." Homi demanded that the company recognize his Labour Federation and withdraw endorsement from Subhas Chandra Bose's old union. There were twenty-four further demands, including wage raises and ten weeks' maternity benefit payments. The company refused his terms. The strikers came back after five days as though nothing had happened, and the management took a deep breath of relief.

In March the old mills were shut down when the firemen on the hand-fired boilers walked out. The rest of the crews reported daily and were paid, part of their wages, of course, going to the strikers. When we tried to operate the old boilers with green hands, we got about 20 per cent of capacity. No more than a few weeks later the finishers in the sheet-mills took a holiday. The company could make black sheets and stock them, but they couldn't galvanize the sheets for shipment. When the old trade union tried to reassert itself and get the men back to their jobs, there was a near-riot, during which the workers heaved buckets of night-soil at their former leaders.

In the meantime, Homi had refused membership in his union to any clerks, thus automatically ruling out the Brahmin element, whom the workers mistrusted. He went to the Government officials and stated unequivocally that the old, company-recognized union cared for nothing but to further its own political aims and that these aims were definitely anti-Government. He pledged his union to co-operate with the Government and to run it along strict trade-union principles.

On June 1, after three months of sitdown strikes, lightning strikes, and general bedlam, the company declared a lock-out. It had become impossible to carry on as things were, and the management decided to use the lock-out period to utilize certain suggestions from the Tariff Board as to the number of men which would be ample to produce all the steel required. Only that number of men would be rehired.

It was an excellent idea—on paper. The hiring was to be staggered. On August 12, coke-oven and blast-furnace men would be taken back, then open-hearth and duplex-furnace men. Later, when all the bad and dubious fellows had been weeded out, the mill men would be permitted to come back. We put desks at the main gate and stationed superintendents behind them with lists of eligible men. We were confident that the workmen had been taught a lesson by two and a half months of enforced idleness.

August 12 arrived, the gates were opened, and not one workman turned up. New, untrained men were brought hurriedly into town. The company finally got a battery of coke-ovens and one blast furnace working. Then two open-hearth furnaces began operating, after a fashion. But still the management refused to have any dealings with Manech Homi and his union.

Eventually, with Subhas Chandra Bose's offer to mediate, a solution seemed to be possible. A whole month went by in arguments and meetings which lasted until morning. Certain demands were met, others rejected. The company recognized the Labour Federation, but refused to disown the old union. In a long list of twenty-four further conditions, the ten weeks' maternity benefits were granted, the strike-pay clause was rejected, and stipulated wage increases were met in part. Another demand was the extension of a loan to the workmen equal to wages lost during the lock-out. This loan was made, with token deductions of one rupee from time to time to keep it alive and to prevent the men from claiming that they had received strike pay.

It was settled that all the men would be taken back except a handful who were accused of sabotage. These were to have hearings. All the superfluous men were to come back and they will be transferred to other departments to fill vacancies. A bond scheme was agreed upon, starting with a monthly production of 30,000 tons. That was where we bogged down once more. For the men didn't want bonuses, but a raise in wages.

Short sitdown strikes retarded production again. The men insisted anew that the company recognize Homi's union, that they would have a bargaining body, without any company officials as members, which would secure for them the same rights as British labour. John C. Peterson in Bombay pointed the way for the local management. Since at least 80 per cent of our labour had embraced the new union under Manech Homi, he said, and the remaining 20 per cent might or might not have confidence in the old union, we should immediately recognize the new one. And since trade unionism was now established, we should recognize any other unions formed in the future to represent other types of labour.

The old union, with Subhas Chandra Bose as president, had never been registered under the Trades Union Act. We did finally, endorse the new group, which Homi immediately registered. But the act empowered the Government to scrutinise the procedure, finances, and expenditures of a union. And Manech Homi, who had prepared so carefully for his career as a labour leader, had one great weakness—he trusted the lieutenants.

During the turbulent years through which the union has been fighting for its life, a regular system of book-keeping would have been a miracle. Men paid their dues on street corners, in the bazaars, in house-to-house canvasses. The collectors were committee members deputized by Homi, and they worked overtime. Some months the collections ran as high as $10,000 for all of which receipts were tendered. The head of a union is responsible for the way it is run. When Homi discovered that his treasurer and the collectors were making a good thing for themselves out of union dues, there were stormy sessions. The news spread through the bazaars. A handful of members petitioned the local government for auditors to go over the union finances.

The auditors found the books in the utmost confusion. They also searched in vain for trace of a considerable sum of money. The treasurer blamed the president and some others. There were many who accused the treasurer. The whole fight went to court and several union leaders landed in jail, including Manech Homi. The union ceased to function. When Homi came out of prison, probably with slightly less faith in his fellow men, a new union sprang up. One of the first clauses in its constitution provided that, "The president can collect and spend up to 100,000 rupees on whatever he wishes. He is not accountable for this sum to anybody."

That union is still running, the legal voice of its many thousands of members. Its history, in a general way, parallels the growth of the whole union set-up in India. It took fifteen years of unrest, of resistance to the reaction of a few employers, of gradually abating extremes on both sides, for Indian labour to accomplish what British labour brought about between 1825 and 1871—the establishment for all time of the principle of collective bargaining.

When the Tariff Board reviewed the steel-industry situation in 1923, they didn't limit themselves to consideration of the benefits of a protective tariff. They strongly recommended that the company spend as much every year in rounding out the plant as they put into their depreciation allotment, about $3,000,000. This was sound, and the company instantly agreed.

Again, three years later, the company and the Tariff Board acted almost together. This time the subject was reduction of fuel consumption. The technical advisor of the Board compared Indian steel-making figures with German ability to produce steel with an even lower coal consumption than the best American or British practice. The advisor urged Tata's to follow German methods and forget both the British and the American. According to him, the United States had so much high-quality, inexpensive coal that American companies didn't have to worry about an extra ton here or there. Americans were extravagant anyway, in steel-making as in endowing foreign missions.

Germany, on the other hand, had lost vast coal reserves with Alsace-Lorraine. She had to use coal frugally or go out of business. We all know Germany made tremendous strides after the first World War. It is not so widely appreciated that she utilized this progress to sell the services of German experts to other countries, and in doing so succeeded in planting highly effective German salesmen where they could profit her greatly.

In 1927, at the annual meeting of the Tata shareholders, the chairman announced that the company had engaged a German fuel-economy expert, with the promise that he would effect a tremendous saving in coal costs. The German had been engaged by a British expert who had just completed an intensive study of German modern scientific management. The Britisher had formerly been chief metallurgist for the Indian Government.

The young Technical Institute boys were now taught that a steel man should go to England, watch steel-plant operation, and see what not to do; he should go to America and learn how to avoid spendthrift practice; then he should go to Germany and see the job done right. We didn't know then just how credulous that English expert was who guided Tata policy.

It is true enough that even today German and Belgian plants are producing steel on a lower B.T.U. consumption than the

Americans do or can hope to equal. It is also true that it costs more to make a Cadillac than a Ford.

American railroads, and American, British, and Indian engineers in general, specify steel made by the open-hearth process. They won't use basic Bessemer steel. There is a reason. Open-hearth is stronger, more resilient. An engineer who designs a bridge plans it to have a margin of safety of seven. If he places a piece of steel that must stand a strain of 100 tons, he uses a beam that will stand up under 700 tons. Further, he specifies steel made and tapped from an open-hearth furnace by the open-hearth process. Acid Bessemer or basic Bessemer might be just as good, but if he wants to be sure and be able to sleep nights, he calls for steel which has passed the highest tests.

Of course, if a man wants to build a dog-kennel, or to fence in a sheep-run or a rabbit warren, he doesn't ask for British or American Standard steel; he takes ordinary untested steel, which is much cheaper. In Europe what he buys would be made by the basic Bessemer process.

Excellent steel can be made in basic Bessemer furnaces. But it takes more time, more care, and yields a lower production. The Tata shareholders were not told all this. Nor were they told that German coal can produce coke of less than 10 per cent ash, while at that time we got from Indian coal coke running as high as 24 per cent. Had our Englishman compared German practice and ours by contrasting available carbon per ton of steel, allowing for the respective amounts required to take care of the differing ash content, he would have been nearer the truth.

The stockholders were presented with but one, misleading fact: that Tata's used three times as much fuel to make a ton of steel as did the Germans. Sir Nowroji Saklatwalla, chairman of Tata Sons, was sold on German efficiency. The Tariff Board technical expert was sold on German methods. We were sold a German bill of goods; fuel engineers, economy engineers, draftsmen, librarians, instructors for the Technical Institute, arrived in numbers from Germany, all of them equipped with German textbooks.

After they had settled in and begun to make their weight felt, I wrote to Sir Nowroji in detail of my distrust of the new set-up and the reasons for it. I remembered "Guts" Myers; I remembered the night in the fall of 1914 when the Tata Germans were bundled into a train and whisked off to a prison camp. I remembered, too, the furnaces in the Ruhr Valley for which the Germans had made such unfounded claims. Sir Nowroji replied that I was old-fashioned. I should try not to be anti-German just because I was pro-American.

Sir Nowroji Saklatwalla died before the war was declared in 1939. He wasn't there in Jamshedpur to see the special railway cars filled up with German key men from Tata's only a few weeks after the war started, to see the train pull out for a remote place far away from the plant already preparing to roll out munitions for the Allies.

As for American steel men being extravagant, I can't see it. Their reputation for being so is part of clever German propaganda. Back in the ancient-history days of 1910 in Gary we were turning out open-hearth quality steel on a low fuel consumption. If I've got the figures right, we got 3600 tons of pig-iron a day from eight furnaces with a coke consumption of 3600 tons. We produced about 22,000,000 cubic feet of blast furnace gas an hour. We utilized it this way: 30 per cent for heating the blast; 12½ per cent for blowing engines; 2½ per cent for gas washers; 7½ per cent for boiler fuel; 45 per cent for power-house gas engines; 2½ per cent loss.

Coke-oven gas produced 50 per cent of the steel ingots; the surplus, above requirements for heating the coke-ovens, was used in the mill-heating furnaces. Roughly 450 lb. of coal per ton was needed to produce the other 50 per cent of steel ingots. From this, Gary's coal consumption was around 1.5 tons of coal per ton of finished product. And this was in 1910.

The basic Bessemer furnaces in Germany require 1.15 tons of iron to make a ton of ingots, using 1.15 tons of good coke. The carbon, silicon, manganese, phosphorus, and a small percentage of the iron itself are burned up in the converters. No outside fuel is needed. The blast-furnace and coke-oven gas can be used in gas engines and mill-heating furnaces. If more fuel is required, there are usually coke-ovens near by or accessible. Gas produced during the week-ends is customarily piped to huge reservoirs and used up during the week.

And whereas the Germans installed meters and gauges in all consuming departments to show them at a glance where the fuel was being utilized or wasted, the Americans first developed carburettors which would burn their gases efficiently. Then they installed gauges as a check. And the same Germans who accused U.S. steel men of extravagance were charging their furnaces with enormous quantities of scrap, steel scrap as well as iron, when the American and Indian mills were making pig-iron direct from iron ore.

Some 47 per cent of all fuel charged into a blast furnace is utilized in reducing iron oxide to metallic iron. Of course, a man can brag about low fuel consumption if he charges metallic iron instead of ore. But is it economical to turn steel back into pig-iron and then reduce the pig-iron to steel again?

Part of the German high-pressure salesmanship consisted in offering machinery and equipment on a barter basis. They were even willing to make a 15 to 30 per cent reduction on tender prices. One of the star salesmen maintained in India knew we were in the market for a certain small metallurgical plant, on which we planned to spend about $150,000. This German advised us not to bother getting out a specification for the plant. His firm had just completed contracts to finish similar plants in Germany and Czechoslovakia.

He flew to Germany the next day and three weeks later returned with blueprints and specifications and offered to let us use them in calling for tenders. We actually gave the contract to a New York firm, but we felt so sorry for the German engineer that later we threw half a dozen jobs his way. In the end, his firm made more money from us than if they had won the big job. The new crop of Germans were not only experts in their own lines. They went in for good golf and tennis. They were welcomed at the club and saw to it that they made a lot of friends.

One of them, a man who had been our chief draughtsman before the first World War, was foreign sales engineer for a large German steel company. He arranged it so that our Technical School graduates went to Germany instead of to America. The United States depression had made it difficult to place our young men in American industry. Now the yearly exodus of boys went to Krupp's, Demag's, and Thyssen's works, and the Germans were careful to treat them royally. When the lads came back to India, they were so many more salesmen for anything German.

When the present war broke out, Tata's were spending some $2,000,000 less a year in the United States than they had, and that much more in Germany. In 1936 a German firm secured a contract for $5,000,000 worth of coke-oven installations. The previous contract, for $3,000,000, had gone to the United States. Aside from the General Electric Company, American firms were finding it hard to sell India as much as a feed-water pump. I think it's fairly certain that had there been no war, by 1945 the Indian steel industry would have been buying only German equipment.

There was a saying in Rome 1900 years ago referring to Agrippina, wife of the Emperor Claudius and daughter of Germanicus, "Nothing good ever came out of Germanicus".

Even the present war will make a difference only for a while. Indian trade will go back to Germany, unless a wise policy prevails in the United States. American chemical and metallurgical manufacturers could easily absorb every year thirty or more young Indians with technical degrees, train them for a year or two for a nominal salary, or none at all, and send them back to India. Undoubtedly they would boost American methods.

In 1933, when the new German contingent had got well into their stride, the company began having a new kind of trouble. The Tariff Board's idea that the shareholders should wait for their dividends until the company was once more at high peak of efficiency didn't go so well with the shareholders. The Tariff Board had ordered the company to put its house in order. Tata's were doing just that. The chart shows that it was only after the protection period that returns began to pour in. But for quite a while the general meetings were stormy. The management, the directors, the agents—everybody in sight had to learn how to take it, from the shareholders and from the Press. Only an earthquake restored the company's prestige as a national asset.

During the hot noon hour most of us took a siesta, not sleeping, but stretched out under a fan in something cool. One day my wife was reading on one bed and I was studying *Racing Form* on the other. Suddenly my wife landed on the floor. She was pretty cross. She claimed that in an access of playfulness I had pushed her off the bed. Then we both noticed the queer stillness of the air. We saw that the large overhead fan was swinging crazily in all directions. There was a deep rumble in the earth beneath us. We rushed into the garden. During the afternoon everyone spoke of the tremor. But mild earthquakes were fairly frequent, and we thought nothing of it.

At nine o'clock that night I received a telegram from Sir James Sifton, Governor of Bihar and Orissa: "Northern Bihar and entire Ganges Valley devastated by earthquake stop can you help with doctors, nurses, medical supplies, clothing, galvanized sheets, light structural steel for temporary hospitals, men stop most urgent."

The deputy commissioner of the district, "Dead-eye" Davis, arrived on the heels of the messenger. Together we went to work, Dead-Eye on one telephone getting me "line clear" on all the phones and telegraph lines in Bihar and Orissa, I on the other, summoning a dozen key men from the plant, the local grain merchants, and all available doctors. We got hold of Alec Duncan of the Bengal-Nagpur Railway in Calcutta. He put a special morning train to north Bihar at our disposal with right of way even over the mail trains. Alec also arranged for a special freight train to start at once and pick up rice from the godowns along the railroad. We worked all night.

By eight the next morning we dispatched the relief train from Jamshedpur. It carried fourteen doctors, six nurses, a carload of blankets, bandages, and medicine, and a complete field operating theatre. Other cars carried loads of angles, small beams, bolts, nuts, and rivets, 400 tons of galvanized sheets, and 200 tons of rice. A dozen European and American engineers, one hundred expert mechanics under the Government metallurgical inspector, Pop Wraight, and Tata's welfare superintendent, Kish Nowroji, set off on a circuitous route for Monghyr, the epicentre of the earthquake. It took them twenty-four hours to get there, twenty-four hours of detours around devastated areas, sometimes on foot, and of being shunted around huge new crevasses.

Within a day of the arrival of the relief train, a temporary hospital had been thrown up and housed more than 400 patients. Each day thousands of people were inoculated for cholera, smallpox, and tetanus.

Lord Willingdon, who was then Viceroy, jumped into a plane in Delhi and got to Monghyr just as the relief staff was getting under way. The town was in ruins. But there, as if by magic, stood a functioning hospital on one side, and on the other a sheltered enclosure where the homeless were being fed. He wired me, "Tata's have done splendidly. Willingdon."

Immediate needs were met immediately, but there were preventive measures to be taken besides inoculation of the survivors. The hundreds of dead had to be removed to prevent epidemics. Wrecking squads formed of volunteers extricated whole families buried beneath their fallen houses. Many of them were still alive. But the ones who were not had to be removed instantly. The dead decompose quickly in India. One old woman had died, buried under a pile of rubble and debris from the breasts down. The wrecking crew slipped a rope around her chest under the arms to pull her out. They were extremely gentle, but at the first slight tug on the rope, her body fell apart below the ribs.

Fifteen thousand people lost their lives in that earthquake. For miles around the soil was covered with salt water and sand. A well-driller told me he had struck a stream of brackish water 40 feet deep some 400 feet below the surface of the Ganges Valley.

Thousands of persons were undoubtedly saved by the prompt succour of the Tata Iron and Steel Company. Tata's contributed supplies and the services of its technicians without thought of recompense, just as the railroad had provided transportation.

The company gave generously, too, to the earthquake fund. Two Englishmen and one Indian from Tata's, who had been on the distress crew, received honours the following June on the King's birthday. But more important, all India suddenly realized anew the value of the company in times of need, that indeed Tata's was not out to exploit the country, but to benefit it. The grumbling of the shareholders was replaced by a rightful pride in their company.

Perhaps the largest private contributor to the earthquake relief fund was Indra Singh, the same modest man who had walked forty miles to take his first job with Tata's at thirty-seven cents a day. He had become Jamshedpur's leading citizen, and amassed a fortune as a labour contractor by paying the highest wages and getting the best possible conditions for the thousands of men and women on his pay-roll. We came to depend heavily on the man. Once when the monsoons had flooded out the tracks and railway traffic was tied up for days, he had thrown his whole organization into the loading of the 1500 tons of iron ore a day, 1000 tons of limestone, and 2000 tons of coal needed to augment the supply of the company's steam-shovel crew. Whenever there was a shortage of raw materials, or a flood, or a strike, the management chorused, "Send for Indra Singh!"

It so happened that Tata's had never built a rod-mill. One of Indra Singh's first independent ventures was to buy the Indian Wire Products Company from the debenture-holders. Tata's promised to supply him up to 4000 tons of billets a month if he would put up a rod-mill. He sent one of his sons to Germany. The lad brought back a mill complete with furnaces and the operators to run the plant. This was a couple of years after the earthquake. Singh floated a limited company with shares at a par of 100, retaining 50 per cent of the stock. Six months later the shares stood at 600.

This Sikh gentleman had started out with only the equivalent of a grade-school education and the natural endowments of intelligence, honesty, and ambition. While many other Indians spent their days bewailing the Indian lot and grumbling against the Government, a few like Indra Singh showed what could be done if a man put his mind to it.

Two energetic Indians, a Punjabi named Agawalla and a Bengali named Rachitt, took over a property which had been abandoned by some nervous financiers and started a cast-iron works, the Tatanagar Foundry Company. They divided India's railway-sleeper business with Tata's. Metal sleepers, or ties, were a godsend to India, for even after chemical treatment a wooden sleeper is the prey of termites, particularly in tropical countries. If a railroad specified rolled-steel sleepers, they came from Tata's. If they wanted cast-iron ties, the Tatanagar people gave them good ones which passed the strict British Standard: Specifications. But although Tatanagar's branched out into diversified foundry castings for engineers and enlarged their plant, they never employed an engineer who was not an Indian.

Except for a small amount made by a plant near Bombay, and the tools fashioned crudely for their own use by the little primitive iron-workers in the hills of Orissa, not so long ago all of India's agricultural implements were imported from Sheffield in England. The supplying of these items in the East is a fairly complicated affair. A pick, shovel, hoe, or rake may be perfect for the workers in the tea-gardens of Assam, and be almost unsaleable in the tea-gardens of Ceylon, or the Indian paddy-fields. Each district has its own ideas of the right shape for a shovel or a pick, and will have none of any other.

The Agricultural Implements at Jamshedpur was built to turn out 4000 tons of tools a year, but seldom made more than 1000 tons, not only because of the stiff foreign competition, but because they refused to cater to district preferences. The company staggered along for a few years. Then Tata's took it over and brought out from England E. G. Price, who knew the Indian market well. The Tatas and Price scrapped a lot of the original tooling machines and installed new and more varied dies. Before long the plant had to be enlarged because production had grown from 40,000 tools to 300,000 a month. Now, of course, the company is working full-out on munitions.

One plant, the smallest industry in Jamshedpur, was created to utilize an inconvenient by-product. Before black-iron sheets can be galvanized, they have to be thoroughly pickled in sulphuric acid to remove all impurities. Then the waste acid must be disposed of. We flushed it down a soil-pipe leading to an open drain which carried waste water back to the river. But the drain ran through some fields where cattle grazed. Once in a while the cattle would drink some of the acid-contaminated water and die. The Government got after us. Tata's incorporated the Tatanagar Chemical Company, erected a plant, and impounded the waste water and acid in small reservoirs. They hired an English chemist, who took over, removed the acid, and used it to produce red oxide paint.

The engineer fellow who managed the business was an Englishman who had lived a long time in Central Africa. He was a top-notch polo player, but he had one or two eccentricities. For one thing, he preferred to live in a tent rather than a house. For another he had a pet which used to curl up on the foot of his bed at night and watch over him as he slept. This pet was a fourteen-foot rock python.

The English have long been accused of being slow and hide-bound, of muddling through. I recall one case when the Indian Government out-muddled anything you have ever heard about the English. And made fools of themselves in the doing.

Some years ago the Indian Government realized that while India could produce her own railroad rails and fish-plates, and she could make freight-cars with her own steel, she had no plant for the manufacture of locomotives. During the first World War a lot of stuff intended for India went to the bottom in transit, including an unrevealed number of railway engines. The Government issued a *communiqué* stating that tenders would be invited annually for all the railway locomotives and boilers required during the twelve years commencing with 1923. They estimated the annual purchase of 400 locomotives and the same number of boilers.

The British acted with dispatch. Six months later the Peninsular Locomotive Co., Ltd., was incorporated in Jamshedpur with a subscribed capital of $2,000,000. There were four Indians on the board of seven under Herbert L. Reed, who was also chairman of the board of Kerr, Stuart and Company, established English locomotive engineers. Tata's agreed to furnish raw materials and cheap power and water to the new subsidiary. The Peninsular people dismantled large buildings in England and got them shipped over and ready by the time the foundations were dry. It was a solid venture, with the presumable backing of the Government. Yet it never produced a single locomotive.

The company heads decided that although they were promised sale of 400 locomotives a year, in order to operate economically they should keep their capacity down to 200 units a year to begin with.

That was the era during which India was overrun with committees and commissions. Whenever a Government department or action came under fire from the public, a commission would be appointed to look into it and thus the day of reckoning postponed for a couple of years. This time it was the railways. They weren't producing enough revenue. The Inchape Committee arrived from England to "investigate". The result was a recommendation that instead of buying new locomotives, India make better use of the ones already in use. Electrification of the roads near Bombay was to release another 300 locomotives for use in other parts of India. So, instead of the estimated 400 new locomotives a year, the Peninsular Company was told that no more than 100 would be needed in any one year.

They went to the Tariff Board for protection. And were told that since the Indian market was restricted, the overhead charges alone would so load the industry that locomotive manufacture would not prove a commercial proposition. The Board did, however, recommend "special consideration" by the Indian Government and agreed to some compensation. There were the usual lengthy negotiations and the thing promised to drag on indefinitely, until one peppery gentleman threatened to buy the front page of the London *Times* and publish all the relevant letters of the Government. He meant it, too. Compensation was promptly forthcoming.

Of late years there has been a minor manufacture of certain limited types of railway engines. But they are a very small drop in a very large bucket. Today, when they can't get them at any price, the Indian railroads would pay a king's ransom for a few first-class locomotives. And this ridiculous and unnecessary shortage is entirely the fault of the near-sighted policy of the Indian Government.

To establish and maintain an empire in India, the Moghuls built roads and bred plenty of tough, fast horses. Akbar could not have restored and consolidated that empire throughout northern India if he had not been a road-builder. The British built roads, too, and implemented them with rails of steel and trains that in normal times carried 500,000,000 people a year. Now, when the vitally necessary transportation of troops and supplies taxes the railroads almost unbearably, there are not enough modern engines to pull these trains. And locomotives are as essential to the defence of a country as are fleets of ships and airplanes.

CHAPTER X

MYTHS AND MISSIONARIES

GIN BILL WAS a man full of surprises. We made many trips together, in England and in India, and I was continually discovering new things about the man. I came into my bungalow in Jamshedpur one night to find Bill reading a first edition on Boswell's *Life of Samuel Johnson*, with one side of the volume propped up on a first of Browning's *The Ring and the Book* and the other side resting on Edgar Wallace's *The Ringer*. In all the years I had known Bill, he had never revealed any particular knowledge of Johnson. Now we started a talk that lasted for hours about Hester Thrale, little Fanny Burney, Joshua Reynolds, and the other Johnson friends.

Gin Bill also bore a charmed life. If cheating death is living on borrowed time, Bill was Time's biggest debtor. He had extended the debt uncountable times, in France, in Mesopotamia, on the Afghan border near the savage Khyber Pass, in more than one bout with the bottle. On a trip to Noamundi near the ancient Joda mines, the cool air of the relatively high altitude made Bill sleepy early one night. He picked up a lantern and started for his bedroom just as our mining engineer looked down at the floor near Bill's slippered foot and bare ankle.

He shouted, "Look *out!*" loud enough to startle us both out of our skins. Bill jumped half-way into the room. Where he had been a second before there was coiled an eighteen-inch krait, commonly called a "minute" snake by Indians. This is a misnomer. A man does not die in one minute after being bitten by a krait; it takes fifteen or twenty minutes.

Bill was not disturbed by his close escape. At any rate, not too disturbed to sit with us for a while and quench a newly aroused thirst. Somehow, when Gin Bill had swallowed a double of gin or of scotch, he looked less and less over his shoulder. He could forget then the whispering voice that haunted him. And even though after that few hours of peace Bill knew there would be a night and a morning of reckoning, for a while it didn't seem important.

Bill liked to sit around in the club-house after a round of golf and talk. His favourite theme was that great fighters, and men in general, were mediocre. They became great only in their ability to adapt themselves to their environment. Bill claimed that had Napoleon lived again during the first World War, he would immediately have mastered trench warfare, bettered the campaign strategy, and ended the whole business in a short time. I took the other side, just for the argument, citing Tom Paine, not to mention Abraham Lincoln, both of whom were great because they did not adapt themselves to the current thinking of their time.

Gin Bill had lived so many years on borrowed time that it was hard for us who had known him to believe it when finally the note was called. Even then it took six strong orderlies to keep him in his hospital bed. In death Bill shared the fate of another gifted soldier who also died in delirium tremens, Alexander the Great.

Bill passed on just before we were to set out for the United States together. Fie had never been there, although we had planned the trip many times. I was going on to attend the Iron and Steel Institute meeting in New York, as well as for a change of scene.

Before the first World War, American steel men had no holidays. They worked alternating shifts of ten and fourteen hours, with the famous twenty-four-hour-shift in between. Sunday was like any other day, as a rule. Superintendents took a few days off now and then, but only to visit other plants in the Pittsburgh or Youngstown districts. A steel man never got away from steel.

When automobiles came into general use, the Pittsburgh crowd used to take a trip every year for a week or so up the Mahoning Valley, on what was called the Glyden tour. They visited other plants of their companies and sometimes plants operated by competitors. They swapped ideas. Improvements in plant practice were shared with men from competing firms. The Glyden tours developed a new camaraderie among steel men, led and encouraged by the Carnegie Steel group.

The tours were not entirely devoted to work. And sometimes the play was as rough as the lives of the men who enjoyed it. One year the crowd was entertained at a lavish dinner by the manager of a steel plant who didn't drink. There was plenty of excellent food at the feast, but accompanied only by ginger ale and sarsaparilla. The next year when they were invited to visit his plant and dine with him there was a hard-working furnace man along who figured out what seemed to him a wonderful practical joke.

The entertainment started out with an elaborate lunch held in the host's pretentious home, modelled on a plantation manse. The architect had plainly never heard of John Ruskin, for there were Corinthian pillars in the centre, the corner ones were Roman, and the arch was Doric. The prankish furnace man was irked by both the mansion and its owner, whose strongest tipple was well-watered claret. During the course of the luncheon the furnace man arranged to have a few sticks of dynamite placed strategically under the disharmonious pillars and lighted. There was a terrific, deafening blast and the architect's error was erased. That was also the end of the Glyden tours.

The men in the Chicago district, too, used to get together every year to compare notes on their furnace troubles. Then they had a banquet. One party was entertained by a group of eight lovely young dancers. About two yards of cloth would have made the costumes for all eight of them. When their number was over, the dancers mistook the exit door and streamed out into the lobby, flushed and laughing, and next to naked. A columnist for one of the Chicago dailies happened to see them. During the domestic rows caused by the next day's paper the poor steel men had so much explaining to do that the meetings were called off for some years.

When the U.S. Steel Corporation was formed, the chairman of the board, Judge Elbert Gary, started what were called the Gary dinners. These gatherings were suspected by the Washington trust-busters to be price-fixing sessions. In reality, they provided the only chance the big fellows and the little fellows in the steel game had to meet and talk business. From them grew the American Iron and Steel Institute, patterned after the English Institute.

It was for one of the semi-annual meetings of the Institute that I went West the month Gin Bill died. I was the guest of Tata's first general manager, Bob Wells, then vice-president of the Steel Company of Canada. During the week of the Institute meetings, the boys worked almost as hard as they played. When they finished work, they were thirsty. An old friend from India came up to Bob in the lobby of the Biltmore and asked where he could get a drink.

Bob said, "If you take an elevator to the fifth floor, you'll be asked into every room as you pass. The same goes for any floor up to the twenty-fifth."

After the banquet which climaxed the week, everybody kept open house. A lot of blast-furnace men foregathered in a Youngstown man's room. The talk swung to the furnaces of the future. Somebody produced crayons, and soon three of the walls were covered with designs. Herman Brassert, the top-ranking engineer of the day, prophesied a twenty-eight-foot-diameter furnace. It wasn't more than two years later that a twenty-eight-foot hearth furnace went up in Pittsburgh. Herman and I became friends at that meeting. Nine years later he turned up in India. While he was there he designed a new furnace for Tata's, which came into operation two years ago and is averaging 11000 tons a day on about 1800 lb. of coke per ton of iron.

Engineers are supposed to be cold, matter-of-fact men who carry slide rules in their pockets and an engineering handbook in their overnight bags. Actually, most great engineers are emotional and given to day-dreaming. There's a lot of poetry in a steel bridge spanning a wide river, a huge, symmetrical blast furnace, a long roll train in a sheet mill, the rolls synchronized to the fraction of a second. Few engineers will admit it, but many of them are as temperamental as opera singers.

When Herman Brassert landed in Bombay in 1937, he expected and wanted to find the India of Kipling. He went to the Taj Mahal Hotel, a Tata project, to a suite not unlike one he would have had at the Carlton in London, except for the whirling electric fan in the ceiling. He dined in the air-conditioned dining-room to the music of a Viennese orchestra. He travelled across India to Calcutta in an air-conditioned train as comfortable as the Twentieth Century Limited. From Calcutta he was whisked to Jamshedpur in a Tata plane in less than an hour. A Rolls-Royce took him to the company guest-house, where he sat on a divan made in Michigan, rested his feet on a Persian rug, found relief from the heat in a drink made in Scotland served by a Hindu bearer, while a Mohammedan followed up with a bottle of Schweppes.

He looked around for a while. Then he said, "I've been in this country for more than a week. And I'd like to know, where *is* India, anyway?" We took him to see the village of the ancient iron workings at Joda. And to Noamundi. He saw thousands of little Indians attacking open mining-faces and loading the ore into mining-tubs. Twenty diminutive locomotives whistled and shrieked as they pulled the cars down to the crushers. There the larger lumps of ore were reduced and passed down into modern sixty-ton hopper cars below, ready to be sent off to the Tata furnaces at Jamshedpur. He saw endless streams of Kohl, Santal, and Ho women, the inhabitants of the district, walking in a steady line from the mining faces to the narrow-gauge track with baskets of iron ore balanced on their heads.

Herman marvelled at the thickness of the iron ore veins and the exceedingly high quality of the ore. He complimented the engineers, all but one of whom were Indians, on the appearance of their mine and workings. If Indian iron deposits had been hidden deep in the earth, as were many veins in eastern Pennsylvania and New Jersey, it would be more understandable that the country did not develop into a steel producer in pre-modern times. But huge deposits of nearly pure iron oxide thrown up by volcanic action millions of years ago, lay barely covered with soil in highly visible hills. Villagers living near these deposits have been picking up float ore and turning it into rustless columns and forgings since before written history. How is it possible, then, that the presence of the ore could have remained almost unknown until comparatively recently?

Megasthenes, the Greek, wrote of having seen iron workings in India in 302 B.C. Four centuries before Christ, King Chandra Gupta had an official whose title was Superintendent of Mines. And we learn that his chief duty was to make borings beneath the surface wherever the presence of slag or ashes indicated "*ancient* workings"! Joda is situated in the heart of what was Chandra Gupta's kingdom. The little hillmen of the village had been working with ore thousands of years before Gupta's time, yet the knowledge of the rich veins was lost to all the rest of the world until Jamshedjee Tata's prospectors found the village and the mine.

The happy, friendly little hillmen fascinated Herman Brassert as they had fascinated me. Their lives, with a simple, unvarying history of birth, marriage, procreation, and death, are full and complete. No diversions, as we know them, are needed to break the monotony of living; indeed, I doubt that it is monotonous. If there is any such thing, the little men of Joda are the never-changing East. They challenge the accepted belief that what we call civilization, with its perfection of mechanics, its emphasis on material improvements, is necessarily a boon. Uncomplicated, "uncivilized" peoples are not so concerned with competition, with getting ahead of the other fellow, as to forego meditation and the search for immortality. If Heaven lies about us in our infancy, surely the little Joda men are closer to God than many of us who view the world from the sixtieth floor of an office building.

So, too, with the benefits that conversion to Christianity is popularly supposed to hold for the ancient peoples of India. We are often told that the abyss which separates Hindus and Mohammedans can be bridged only by imposition of the Western faith. But is the East really "never-changing", or is the West changing so fast that it is only by comparison that the East seems to stand still? And I have often wondered if the West is as Christian in fact as in name.

Many sincere people believe that it is time for the West to step in and take charge of the spiritual life of the Indians, to salve them from destroying themselves with their new industrial playthings. This well-meant philosophy only makes Indians smile. They read of the rescuing effect Christianity is exerting on Indian thought. Yet they also hear and read many things about present-day Western civilization which cause them to appreciate in many ways their own superiority.

One sentence in *Rethinking Missions*, published in the United States in 1932, aroused widespread resentment among intelligent Indians: "Christianity will supply the remedial palliative needed by the wounds of modern industry. Otherwise the culture of poor India will perish." Many Indian readers dropped the book after reading that sentiment expressed so baldly, so condescendingly. So Hinduism and the faith of Islam must give way to Western creeds if modern industry is to continue enriching modern Indian life! Indians can be cutting and to the point. They remarked that at least rackets and night clubs have not yet appeared in their "poor" culture.

I have met many real Christians in India. They happened to be Hindus and Mohammedans, but in spirit they were more Christian than a number of people I have known west of Suez.

I am reminded of a funeral in India. A European friend of mine had died. I was standing over him when the doctor dropped his hand. Suddenly the man fought and breathed again for a few seconds. Then he went out. It was eleven o'clock. Five hours later, so as to bury him before sundown, we took his remains to the Catholic church. Among the other pall-bearers there were a Parsi, a Hindu, a Brahmo-Samaj, a Mohammedan, and a Sikh. Both

Brahmo-Samajis and Sikhs profess a reformed creed of Hinduism. During the service all of them knelt with bowed heads, the Mohammedan perhaps bending lower than the rest.

Not long ago, in a Western city, I saw another funeral procession passing into a church. The coffin contained the body of an old woman who had once been beautiful, vital, and good. I knew the story of her betrayal, of a summer's day some fifty years before, when she and her suitor had yielded to each other by a calm, cool lake, near the tree where their horses were tied. Later, she had borne proof of their common ecstasy, a son, "to suffer like themselves a while, and die". But the man and the woman were of different religious sects. The man disowned the relationship and the child. Now I saw the man, after half a century of irresponsible and unbridled living, walking back and forth in front of the church. He took off his hat, stood irresolute a moment on the steps. Then he replaced the hat and paced once more up and down. He could not go inside to make an honest farewell, for that church and its God was one he had been taught to abhor.

The evening before I had chanced to hear a lecture on India by a woman whose very brief stay there did not, of course, prevent her from knowing all about it. Her theme was that only Christianity could "save" the East. Save it from what, I wondered now, observing this exhibition of spiritual cowardice, and contrasting it with the many examples of brotherly feeling I had often seen displayed by Indians.

One day at Tata's a mixer crane had been hoisting a ladle containing seventy-five tons of molten pig-iron. When the ladle achieved the proper height, the crane men commenced gradually to tip the enormous ladle so that the bubbling stream could flow into the vat, called a mixer, wherein hot metal was stored before it went to the Bessemer converters to be blown into steel. Down below, at what seemed a safe distance, a number of bricklayers were relining other giant ladles.

Nobody knows just what went wrong. But slowly at first the ladle fell away from its supports, then severed itself completely and crashed to the ground, vomiting sparks and burning metal. As the molten iron reached out towards the bricklayers it met and exploded puddles of water. The air was filled with the rending noise of the ladle flinging itself to earth, the confused and frenzied shouts of the men, and the inimical hiss of steam.

By the time I had run for my car, the ambulance had arrived. But it could carry only five, leaving eleven men, dazed with the agony of their burns, on the ground. I could take but three, for fear that skinless bodies placed too close together might adhere one to the other. I had to act quickly, since immediate medical attention was imperative to save any of them. I decided to take the three who seemed to have the best chance of surviving. All eleven were propped in some sort of sitting posture, their eloquent, beseeching eyes unforgettable. I felt that they knew I was pronouncing judgment upon them. If I should pass by a man, his hours were numbered.

I spotted one who had more skin than the others, who could turn his head and follow my movements. Turning to the rescuers, I said in Hindi, "Take him".

The man shook his head in negation. "Do not take me away," he said. He had remembered to use the polite form of the imperative of "to take away".

Turning his head feebly, the Hindu nodded towards the body of a half-burned Mohammedan whose chest was heaving in agony and spoke. *"Hamara bhaiko lejao."*— "Take my brother," he said clearly. The Hindu who was in pain and in danger of death remembered, not that the Mohammedan was of a different faith, but that he was his brother.

I was in Patna once, at the trial of a man who had killed another in front of several witnesses. The prisoner sat in the dock with one leg chained to the floor and an arm fastened to the railing, in case he should try to make a bolt.

All at once the courthouse began to sway alarmingly. We realized instantly that there was a quake. The crowd, including the judge and the prosecuting attorney, rushed down the stairs and out into the courtyard. The ground continued to heave, a heavy piece of cornice fell with a thud, and there was loud rumbling in the earth. The British judge asked the chief of police where the prisoner was. The policeman said, "Don't worry, your Honour, he can't escape. He is chained to his place."

The British judge, the Hindu prosecuting attorney, and the Mohammedan defence lawyer didn't hesitate. They ran back up the stairs, released the prisoner, and brought him to safety. The stairway collapsed as they neared the bottom step. That prisoner was a Sikh.

We hear so much about the disparities between the Christian, Hindu, and Mohammedan faiths, we are apt to forget that they agree on three great fundamentals: the infinite goodness of God, the efficacy of prayer, the love of one's fellow men.

Long before Moses led the Israelites out of Egypt, the Holy men of India and their like in central Asia were studying theology, ethics, logic, and the structure and history of the universe. Nearly forgotten Indian tablets describe the creation of man on the lost continent of Mu, the birthplace of humanity, which lay between Asia and the North and South American continents. Later manuscripts tell of the destruction of Mu, of how the earth's crust was first broken by earthquakes and sank into a fiery abyss. "Then the waters of the Pacific rolled in over her, leaving only water where a mighty civilization had existed." An unknown number of years afterwards, in the fourth century B.C., Plato mentioned the land of Mu.

There is the beautifully depicted Hindu concept of the earth as an inverted bowl, supported on five golden elephants standing equidistant on the back of a turtle.

Each of the races of man has had its World Tree. Persian legends centre about the *haoma* tree; the Russians believed there was an iron tree whose root was the "power of God". The Hindu dead clung to the *jambu*, or rose-apple tree, on which they climbed to immortality. Long before Troy existed, India had her sacred fig or banyan tree, called the Tree of Many Feet, since its seed rarely roots in the ground, but sends down hanging gardens of roots from a nest in the crown of a palm. The roots then sink into the earth and spring up from it again, only to send down other drooping branches that in turn root themselves. So one banyan tree makes a whole grove, all part and fibre of the one seed, which eventually crowds out and destroys the palm whose topmost branches once sheltered its beginnings.

Long ages before Troy, Hindu philosophers prayed to God to remove the sinfulness of man. They preached that by living according to God on the earth, a man will be rewarded after a great enough number of good men have died and are secure in Heaven. Then God can be persuaded by prayer to destroy the sinful earth. To some westerners the idea of prayer after death is shocking. They say that God has a will of His own and needs no prompters. They don't, however, hesitate to ask him for worldly favours, even small ones, such as to let them draw the winner in the Derby Sweep.

The same westerners who point out that Mohammed plagiarized some of his teachings from the Bible, neglect to mention that the Jews who wrote the Bible poached some of their beliefs from the Hindus.

The philosophy taught by the Hindus today, just as it was before young Tutankhamen was placed in his tomb, is still sound. Our understanding of it is often obscured by the myths that surround those ancient teachings, because so many of them are clothed in proverbs and allegories. Within, one finds the kernel to be good. The foreigner too frequently sees only the allegory. It is, however, much the same as with our own teachings of mythology. Back of all the legends of the gods and goddesses who held court on Mount Olympus we find, if we take the trouble to probe a little, the true beliefs of early man.

Many dimly imagined æons must have passed before mankind was mature enough to formulate for himself the definite concepts of his own continuity contained in racial myths and legends. And when the wiser among them felt impelled to teach their fellows, they chose the parable to carry their message, as did Jesus of Nazareth.

There is less difference than one might imagine, too, in the Oriental instruction of the young. Christian children are taught to admire the exploits of St. George with the dragon, and that David did a great job with his sling-shot. Hindu children learn of King Janaka's daughter, Sita, who was miraculously born of a field furrow in the twelfth century before Christ. To this day Sita remains to millions of Indians the ideal of female love and devotion. Her story and that of her heroic husband, Rama, is told in one of the two great Hindu epics, the *Ramayana*.

Students may have changed since my day, but I remember the boys at Boston Latin School devouring Bulfinch's *Age of Fable*. And I've never heard a preacher, deploring the Hindu devotion to mythology, who protested the teachings about Psyche and

Eurydice, Hero and Leander, the Roman Shewolf, Aeneas, the love of Anchises for Venus and their resulting offspring, and hundreds of other tales of ancient Greece. The *Iliad* is as much a battle between the gods and goddesses as between the Greeks and the Trojans. I always noticed that the minute a favourite of one of the female Olympians went down for the count, the goddess materialized, armed with a smoke screen, and rushed the recumbent hero off to his bed, to sprinkle him with a handful of water from the Lethe.

India is rich in having two immortal epic poems. The *Ramayana* has something in common with the *Odyssey*. Its story of tribulation and endurance stems from two highly cultured tribes, the Kosslas of Oudh and the Videhas of north Bihar, who had celebrated universities, and whose researches eleven centuries before Christ into the mystery of the soul and belief in one Universal Soul were written down about 800 B.C. and have come down to modern India in the *Upanishads*. The Indian ideals of life—piety, endurance, and devotion—find voice in the *Ramayana*, in contrast, for instance, to the Greek ideals of joy and beauty. But neither Indian epic alone gives the full picture of the ancient Indian mind, for while the *Ramayana* paints its domestic and religious aspects, the *Mahabharata* is a truly heroic tale of valour, ambition, and lofty chivalry....

As for binding Hindu and Mohammedan together by means of Christianity, the gifted Indian teacher Kabir conceived of uniting them in the worship of one God during the fourteenth century. "The God of the Hindus," he said, "is the God of the Mohammedans, be he invoked as *Rama* or *Ali*." And further, "The city of the Hindu God is Benares, and the city of the Mohammedan God is Mecca, but search your hearts and there you will find the God both of Hindus and Mohammedans... if the Creator dwells in tabernacles, whose dwelling is the universe?"

Two hundred years after those words were uttered, the ancestors of Christian missionaries who today speak proudly of stamping out Hindu superstition in India were burning at the stake old women whose only fault was that they were toothless. They probably had pyorrhæa, but to the Puritans they were witches.

Down to the present day in India the popular mind, worshipping many images in many temples, still holds fast to the fundamental idea of one God, of whom the heroes of the epics, *Krishna* and *Rama*, were incarnations. The various sects quarrel over the name by which the Deity shall be known, but in the teeming villages of Bengal, in the ancient shrines of northern India, and far away in the towns of southern India, the prevailing faith is a monotheism which underlies all the diverse ceremonials.

For seven of my twenty-five years in India I was able to meet my leading Mohammedan townsmen frequently and fairly intimately. They had collected a large sum of money with which to build a mosque. Different groups among them disagreed on the site, and no site any of them had selected was suitable to the Government and the company, since they were either near a Hindu temple, in a section where a number of Sikhs resided, or in the centre of the town where a bank was planned. Sir Abdul Aziz, later Prime Minister of Bihar, tried vainly to bring the factions together. Then, for a number of years, I sat in the chair and held the balance, offering a compromise location. My Mohammedan colleagues trusted me, not because I was general manager of the steel company, but because my wife was a daily communicant in the Roman Catholic faith, and therefore I could not be wrongly advised. Yet Mussulmen are often accused of being bigoted.

Calling a man a bigot, like indiscriminate tar-brushing with any of the epithets fashionable from one period to another, is an easy way to avoid really learning something of his beliefs, or of making an honest, balanced judgment. I was once publicly branded as "narrow-minded" by an American missionary on the sole basis of my membership in the Catholic Church. Yet my convictions were formed slowly, and only after years in which I passed through, as have many others, successive stages of doubt, agnosticism, and even licence in thought. I do believe completely in the teachings of St. Paul, and therefore of the Catholic Church. But if my belief were not complete, I would become a Mohammedan tomorrow.

During my long and close association with the Jamshedpur Mohammedans I could not but learn something of their faith. Many of them gave me books about it to read. Sir Aziz presented me with a manuscript copy of the Koran in Arabic, written during the time of Shah Jahan (1628-1658). Yet I cannot pretend to more than a superficial knowledge.

None of the great religions is mastered at a glance. This is realized much more deeply in the East than in the West, for to easterners, and particularly Indians, religion is not something to be professed, but to be lived. They have been amazed and contemptuous to see foreigners on a flying visit to their country go once or twice to a few temples, perhaps the Kalighat temple near Calcutta, watch the slaughter of a few goats sacrificed much as they were when Christ went to the temple in Jerusalem, and then rush into print in America with explanations of the Hindu religion.

Jesuits spend years in study after their contemporaries are judged wise enough to go into the business world to make their fortunes. Prospective Jesuit missionaries are called together two years before they are ready for Holy Orders and asked, "How many wish to join foreign missions in the East? Bear in mind that you will complete your studies out there. And that you will remain at your posts until death."

From among the great number volunteering, only those are picked whose physical stamina is without question. And before they begin their work, they must command an adequate knowledge of general medicine and of agricultural methods and practice.

The Hindu religion is susceptible of intelligent discussion only by the erudite. Really to understand it requires half a lifetime of study and contemplation. A quarter-century of close friendship with Hindus, including much instruction from among their wise men, has left me a respectful, groping yearling. Once when I was younger and rasher, in an article on labour conditions in India I traced some of the causes to the law-giver Manu and made reference to Hinduism. Subhas Chandra Bose wrote from his forced exile in Vienna a scathing criticism of my half-baked views on Hinduism and advised me to stick to my own subject of steel production. In that instance he was quite right.

No man who has not studied and grasped the teachings of Plato and Aristotle should attempt to study Hinduism. And even he can gain only a fair understanding of it—after several years. What little I do know of it includes the fact that, like Christianity, it has a trinity, the triple attributes of the Deity: Brahma, the creator, Vishnu, the preserver, and Siva, the destroyer. For the rest, the most important thing is to observe the effects of Hinduism on human conduct. We in the Christian world are taught to honour our parents. But we too often forget and neglect them. When a Hindu son marries, he only adds a member to the family circle.

One family in Jamshedpur will serve as an example. The father was one of the senior employees of Tata's. Four of his five sons were graduated from the Technical Institute. All five were married. On pay day they turned the whole amount of their earnings over to the patriarch. It was he who suggested new shoes for this one, a new suit for another, or who bought five saris at once for his daughters-in-law. Meals were taken together, at a common table in the large and comfortable house, where they all lived.

I was once asked to take the chair at a lecture given by a Hindu yogi on the infinite goodness of God. It was a hot night, and I hoped the speaker would make his remarks short and to the point. He spoke for three hours, and nobody, least of all I, wanted him to stop. The man had spent five years in absolute silence and meditation. In perfect, uninflected English he spoke eloquently on the inability of the finite mind to comprehend the power and goodness of the Infinite. What race of men could claim that they were preferred above others, he asked, what creed could say that God had inspired its prophets and not all the great teachers of the past, Buddha, Confucius, Mohammed, St. Paul, as well as His own Son?

The Hindu asked me afterwards if he had said anything which would controvert any of the great truths, Christian or other. He had not, and I told him so. "Modern man is too busy with slide rules and balance sheets to spare much time for contemplation," he said. Then he added with a smile, "No doubt God will allow for his foibles."

In normal times Americans pour gold into India every year to maintain and extend the work of their missionaries. Personally I don't think they receive a fair spiritual dividend on their investment. The greatest missionary of all, St. Thomas, went to India at the instance of no generous parish. Today his dust lies buried at Mylapore. But he spread the Word so eloquently that fifteen centuries after his death, Europeans found some one million Christians living on the Malabar coast, people who had long been cut off from any contact with the Western world.

Three of the several fine missionaries I have known in India approached the ideal represented by St. Thomas. They carried out rather literally Christ's admonition to Peter, "Feed my sheep", since a hungry man is more concerned with his stomach than his soul. The first of these three was an Anglican minister who yearly visited a number of communities in Jamshedpur. But he felt he was not doing all he could, he merely repeated the Word to men who should have known it from childhood. He went off to live in the hinterlands with the lowly Santalis and Kohls.

The Anglican had been raised on an English farm. He recalled and increased his agricultural skill. He taught the local Indians how to improve their crops, how to produce lac from certain of their trees. After some years he built a church, then another. And the natives, who had benefited from his earthly wisdom, trusted his spiritual wisdom. They laboured at the building of the churches as devoutly as did the European artisans of the thirteenth century.

The second man was a Texan. He could have inherited a ranch so vast that it was nineteen miles from the gate-posts to the door of the main house. That Texan was a modest man. None of us then knew that his hospital and nurses, his clergy and school teachers in India are all supported from his own pocket.

The third missionary is a Belgian, a priest, who also took up his work in the jungle among the Hos and the Kohls. He taught his flock to rotate their crops and, like Virgil in his *Bucolics*, improved their yield per acre. As an example to his converts, the Belgian went for weeks without tea or coffee, drinking instead a concoction made from the *neem* tree which was not unpalatable and warded off both malaria and dengue fever.

One occasionally meets laymen, too, who work with the true spirit in India. A young American eye specialist went out their for intensive practice in removing cataracts. In a few months he had performed over a thousand operations, most of which were successful. Then he felt he could not go home as long as there was work, and so much of it, to be done. When recurring bouts of malaria forced him to leave, he had never accepted a penny for attending a patient.

I had been in India only a few years when an infected hand made it necessary for me to seek out a doctor in Calcutta, Sir Leonard Rogers. Even with an appointment, I was kept waiting for over two hours while the dozen or so patients before me were taken care of. Finally I went in. The doctor gave every impression of being bored, sitting slumped in his chair and yawning openly in my face. His hair needed cutting and some attention from a comb. The truth was that the man was overworked and exhausted. Eighteen hours of work every day, divided between the laboratory and the clinic, made his personal grooming a matter of no importance whatever.

Rogers was looking for, and later found, cures for both dysentery and leprosy. As a result of his research, intravenous injections have for some time brought relief to thousands of lepers, formerly considered hopeless. Sir Leonard Rogers, too, was a missionary, with his own methods and his own approach. On the day when he examined my hand, he gave me a prescription for stuff to be applied daily.

"What is your fee?" I asked.

"Five guineas if you can afford it. If you can't, there is no charge."

The Sisters of the Church of England are also missionaries. For years they have laboured unselfishly in the hospitals of India. The Presidency General Hospital in Calcutta was built for them. There anyone who needs it receives the same treatment, free, as the affluent British of Clive Street pay through the nose for.

There is no questioning the sincerity of the foreign missionary. There is too often a doubt of his capability. Is he willing to be selfless? Is his wife able to become a good nurse? From what

I have seen, I think that frequently a disproportionate percentage of mission funds is spent in educating the missionary's many children, too much time spent in wiping jam off little Willie's chin. Time which could, for instance, be devoted to nursing a malnourished Indian woman, pregnant with yet another life to add to the already overcrowded community.

The young preacher of an American church once told me that there were not enough Europeans and Americans in Jamshedpur to require the services of an American missionary. Therefore he planned to ask for release, and to suggest instead an Anglo-Indian preacher. He had lived in the community for some time, but he knew less about it than I. He did not know, for example, that there was plenty of work for him to do which could give point and meaning to his weekly sermon.

The Tata Iron and Steel Company's hospital gives free medicine and medical treatment to a million and a quarter people every year, and the Rotary Club had that year devoted its energies to helping the lepers. Yet a late census showed that more than 500 lepers lived in the town and the suburbs of Jamshedpur. That is a high percentage in a town of 100,000 people. Much work, too, lay waiting to be done among the people in promoting preventive medicine. The number of children born sightless because of venereally diseased parents was considerable. Yet talk as much as I liked, I could not convince the young man of God. He refused to believe that such work was fitting to him.

This brings up the question of just who is a missionary. As I see it, a missionary is anyone at all who lives in a foreign country because he thinks he can perform some service for the inhabitants—spiritual, physical, or material. In other words, missionaries, like marriages, are made in Heaven.

One of the most generous, thoughtful and compassionate persons I knew of in India was a woman whose name was a byword along the China Seas—she ran a chain of gambling houses. Like a female Robin Hood, she took money from the wealthy, most of whom she despised, and spent it lavishly on the poor. She paid for the education of promising youngsters, she bought food and clothing, she provided medical care. This woman didn't give a damn about her reputation. To the world she was an enigma and a cynic. She was content to have it so. But a word of thanks from one of the lowly men and women she had helped was enough to bring a flush of pleasure to her face. And I have no doubt that she had less trouble with St. Peter than many of the very righteous who would have refused to take her hand.

No one with eyes could doubt the vast opportunity awaiting the person who wants to work for others in India. On any Sunday, when one leaves any of the always crowded churches, one files between rows of lepers. Some of them have no fingers, or they are lacking a hand or a foot. There stand the sightless too, mute and patient.

There is plenty of work to be done. When the war is won, we should send all the help we can to India, doctors and nurse, engineers and agricultural experts. The men of God who should be especially trained, or they should stay at home. So far, the spiritual and temporal returns from official religion missionaries are nothing to brag about. There are exception. But on the whole we're not getting a fair return on our investment.

There is no such thing as the "unchanging East". The ferment of change, of progress in the political, social, and economy fields disproves that myth conclusively. The people are eager for the Truth, whether it be expressed by the missionary who can wield a plough, a doctor who eases their pain, or an ordain minister who speaks to their hearts.

One Christmas Eve my wife and daughter went with me midnight Mass. Our Afghan driver asked if he might standing the back of the church for the service. I said yes, of course, but that he could hardly get through the crowd, and to come with us through the vestry door. Not only was the church itself packed but the whole churchyard overflowed with natives, many of whom had come on foot from miles away to see the crib and the grotto. The choir was composed of Swiss, Americans, German, Britishers, Spaniards, Dutch, Indians, and Anglo-Indian. The natives were equally conglomerate, of many tribes, costumes, and traditions. They all knelt reverently, touching their foreheads to the floor and raising their calloused hands to God. Our God and theirs, no matter by what name He is called.

CHAPTER XI

INDIAN ARSENAL

THEMSELVES THE DESCENDANTS of invaders, Indians possess timeless quality, not unlike that of the Chinese, which has made it possible for them to absorb various successive invasions and sometimes, to benefit by them. Nobody knows where the Indians who settled in what is now called India started from, but so many time around 2000 B.C. they came through Iran, bringing the Sanskrit language with them; they were Aryans—that the Caucasians, and they drove out the black people they found already inhabiting the valleys and fields of the new land.

For a long time it seemed that every near-by nation felt duty bound to take a wallop at India. After Alexander defeated Porus in 326, there was Ptolemy, among many others, and they all came to raid, to kill and loot, and then swaggered west again with their booty, like the crows in a Calcutta market-place which swoop down on a coolie girl carrying a basket of fish on her head. Since most of the raiders came by land, it was natural that the border tribes should develop into the fiercest fighters. This warlike tradition survives today among the Sikhs, the Punjabis, and other north-western peoples, and is their greatest pride.

Those invaders who came to loot and remained to conquer brought their own contributions to Indian culture. The Moghuls, for example, enriched India with their vitality and imagination. They also brought about a certain measure of new national unity in the north.

The only invaders who have not been assimilated are the British. They created a political stability never before known in India, they initiated immense irrigation projects which have lessened the danger of famines, they have improved communications, schools, and imported public-health measures, but they have not been assimilated. Even cross marriages between Indians and Britishers seem to produce children lacking in both the morals and the graces of either parent.

This is puzzling only if one forgets that the British originally went into India neither to conquer nor to colonize. The charter Queen Elizabeth gave the East India Company granted them only the right to trade, not to colonize. Therefore, because they were only traders, the company's agents could establish themselves in a few fishing villages, like the site of the present city of Madras, and maintain their posts there for nearly a century and a half almost without antagonism.

During that time the political disunity and near-anarchy of the Indian princes became more acute. The same powerful British Navy which could vanquish the French, however, was also able, in time, to impose the will of the East India Company on the country as a whole. This was still not actually a conquest, since many of the Indian princes welcomed British help against their fellows. And close to 90 per cent of the force with which Warren Hastings defeated the Marathas were Indian troops. Modern Japan, continually harping on her "sphere of influence" in the East, undoubtedly has her eye on India's minerals and raw materials, the second most extensive in the world. I am sure that any Japanese invasion of India would eventually be absorbed and would come to nothing. But in my opinion, neither by land nor by sea would such an enterprise be feasible.

It's certainly no news that Japan is and has been for a long while at the Burmese threshold to India, for Akyab is only a long walk to the border. But she would first have to subdue the warlike northern Burmese, who have learned what it means to have exchanged British overlordship for Japanese, and who have been waging a bloody and relentless guerrilla war on the Japanese for some time, although little word of it evades the Japanese censorship. The northern Burmese are mountain fighters like the Serbs, and, like them, don't seem to know that they are "conquered".

Then, even if the Japanese pushed through and secured a foothold in Assam, they would still be far from Calcutta, and Jamshedpur. Not too far for a plane to fly, of course, but I believe that bombing raids on the steel and other industrial plants are unlikely. For one thing, Japan would prefer to have them intact for her own use. But if, knowing at last that she is defeated, she should launch vengeance raids, the considerable Allied air power in India would be able to intercept and smash the bombers before they got near enough to do any damage.

To reach the inland, Japanese troops would have to cross the deltoid plain which straddles the many mouths of the Brahmaputra and the Ganges, a plain ridden with fever, infested with mosquitoes, boggy with marshes, and split with innumerable streams—and one which is approximately 32,000 square miles in area.

If Japan should attempt invasion by sea, she could probably effect easy landings on the numerous sandy beaches along the shore. But there are few harbours on the east coast; and all those deep enough to receive transport ships are well protected by both forts and airfields.

In Bengal, where the people are a fairly emotional lot, there would be the double danger of panic and of fifth-column assistance. Subhas Chandra Bose, the same Bose who once headed the labour union at Jamshedpur, is idolized by the Bengalis. He would be the logical man for the Japanese to put at the head of any invasion force in that direction. The province has, in fact, been swept continually with rumours that such an expedition is actually on the way—with "thousands of Indian troops". Bose has never been known to have Fascist sympathies, so that he would command a trusting, fanatic following in the province. He is not regarded by the Bengalis as a fifth columnist because he, like most of themselves, is not pro-Japanese, but only violently, blindly, and unalterably anti-British.

But again any deeper penetration of the country would bring its own difficulties. For Calcutta lies on the Hooghly River, and the Hooghly is the trickiest water-way in the world. Its bed is continually shifting, from the ceaseless movements of the silt deposited there by torrential rains season after season. It would be simple for the defenders to move the channel buoys. Instantly the river would be unnavigable. And a battleship, so proud a passenger of the seas, is a large and nearly defenceless target for air power once it has run aground on an unexpected spit of land.

All this would not have been quite so true a year and more ago, when India was more vulnerable than we like to remember. Japan's best ally so far has been the element of surprise. Had the Japanese not been held up in Burma, had they not lost valuable time and equipment there, and had they instead struck right through from the east, over the few, bad Burmese roads, through the difficult and mountainous terrain in one long sweep, they might have had considerable success. Then they would probably have been aided by the northern Burmese, who still believed the Japanese had come to free them.

But during the Burma campaign, and in the precious months since, the Indian Army has grown to some 2,000,000 men and has been well supplied with modern guns, tanks, and antiaircraft. There were, in fact, exploratory invasion attacks flung against Ceylon and the east coast of India, and they were defeated.

Indian, British, and American airmen control the air over India. The presence of R.A.F. and U.S. flyers there has been well publicized. It is not so well known that the Indian Army has its own air arm, trained and entirely officered by Indians, which by the end of 1943 will number ten complete combat squadrons. One aviation training-school is located right in Jamshedpur, on the field which used to be our race-track.

Indian cavalry troops have always been among the finest horsemen and fighters. Then there is the small but gallant Indian Navy, whose H.M.I.S. *Bengal*, on convoy duty, covered herself with glory against a strong Japanese attacking force, although she was armed with only one gun and some close-range anti-aircraft. The two sloops, the H.M.I.S. *Jumna* and *Sutlej,* have been transferred from work in the Atlantic to convoy duty in Eastern waters. The numerous craft in the "Silent Service", mine-sweepers and escort ships, are responsible for keeping open the sea lanes to and from Indian ports.

Early in the war India expanded her shipyards and building facilities enormously. There is even an airplane factory, the large Hindustan Aircraft plant at Bangalore, which services ships and at least assembles training planes, fighters, and some light bombers.

In spite of the unrest in India, about which so much is said and so little done, we can take it that the Indian Army is completely loyal. The 250,000 men of overseas detachments, particularly the crack Fourth Indian Division of Montgomery's Eighth Army, have shown what they could do in the most difficult kind of fighting; and before that Indians fought superbly in Hongkong, Singapore, Burma, and Eritrea.

India was taken into the war without her formal consent. But she has made important war contributions other than that of bravery. For the first two and a half years of war in North Africa she was almost entirely responsible for supplying the bulk of stores for use there. Indian industries furnished steel sheds for troop huts, garages, hospitals, and airplane hangars, steel pipes to carry water, thousands of miles of them. She sent locomotives, trucks, wagons, and railway equipment, timber, assault and landing craft; she has developed new manufactures of electric supplies, plastic products, and the vitally needed specific types of batteries for two-way plane-to-ground communication. India made thousands of camouflage nets, some of them hand-woven in the villages. From India came about 90 per cent of the tents to protect troops from heat and machines from sand. She sent food, dehydrated and in bulk, clothing, and even boots expertly made by factory workmen to whom, not long ago, shoes were a novelty.

The scope of India's generous participation in the war is incredible to anyone who knew India only thirty years ago. It is as different from the India of today as the England of Victoria is from the England of Churchill. And not the least factor is that India, by shipping more than 5,500,000 tons of supplies along the fairly open and much shorter route from her ports to North Africa, which would otherwise have had to go all the way from Britain, has saved ships and shipping space for supplies to Russia.

I think old Jamshedjee Tata would be humbly proud if he could know these things, as perhaps he does. For if he and his co-workers had had a little less imagination, a fraction less determination, or even a smaller amount of ability, there might easily have been no Tata's, and probably therefore no steel sheds, no steel water pipes, steel sleepers, steel shells and guns streaming out of Indian ports today.

The whole healthy Indian industrial edifice is built squarely upon the successful manufacture of steel. If she could, Japan would gladly exploit Indian ore, just as she did the ore veins of conquered China and Manchuria. With what she stripped from those territories, her output in 1933 rose from a negligible figure to 2,000,000 tons a year. But long before then Japan had cannily been buying up all the pig-iron she could get, and iron and steel scrap, too.

On a yearly contract basis, she paid Tata's sixty-five rupees a ton for iron alongside steamer at Calcutta, or sixty rupees at work-site. Since we were producing pig-iron for eighteen rupees a ton works cost at the time, it was a nice profit. And it was good iron, better than Japan could produce, with only a small percentage of phosphorus and sulphur. There was profit, as well, in the export of scrap. Japan must now be feeling the loss of those materials, amounting to half a million tons of iron and 300,000 tons of steel scrap, materials which India, like the United States, sent to Japan until, belatedly, the danger was recognized.

The great Japanese weapon in India has been the promise to "free" the Indians. The implications of this promise are not lost on intelligent Indians, or on any Indians at all, for that matter, since the invasion of China. But the desire to be free of the white sahib's smug racial discrimination is close to every Indian's heart.

Perhaps the worst single example of the white man's insistence on his own superiority is furnished by the policy of the Bombay Yacht Club. It stands next to the beautiful archway built in honour of the visit of George V and his Queen in 1912. But although George V was Emperor of India, and the club occupies Indian soil, no Indian is permitted to enter it—except as a servant. The story goes that while the royal party was in Bombay, George V, driving up to the club, accompanied by one of the noblest and richest Maharajas, was told that his Indian guest could not come in !

There is a bar in a corner of the Taj Mahal Hotel which some steel man long ago nicknamed the Snake Pit. One can sit over a drink and watch the sailors, soldiers, drapers' clerks, and so forth dance by with their girls. I was there with a party one night to see the sights. With us we had a brilliant and well-known Indian writer. We got to talking about Home Rule, and I asked him what he would do when it was granted. His clear dark skin flushed and he looked out of the window.

"You can see, as I do," he said, "the lights of the Bombay Yacht Club. The first thing *I* would do would be to put a match to that building with my own hands."

I didn't ask him why. I knew why, only too well.

"That club is a vicious thing," he went on, more calmly. "Noble Britishers are noble indeed, but that club is one of the last strongholds of the East India Company's descendants, the diehards who still think, even now, that India should be ruled with an iron hand and heel."

I thought of the great Willingdon Club, sponsored by one of those truly noble Britishers, Lord Willingdon, when he was Governor of Bombay. Willingdon would allow no discrimination between races, creeds, or colours.

That the Bombay Yacht Club is actually one of the last strongholds of the white man's snobbery towards a race whose civilization antedates his own by several thousand years, is one sign of the changes now taking place throughout India, in many fields. And the country's growing industries are responsible for much of the impetus back of the changes.

An expert industrial technician is any man's equal, in any language. The more need there is for him, the clearer the equality becomes. Industry is also responsible for the falling away of many of the prejudices between Indians themselves. The Hindu who, although terribly burned by liquid metal from the fallen crane, insisted that his Mohammedan brother be saved in his place could have been an exceptional type, but he was not. I have seen frequent proof that the old caste barriers are breaking down—high-caste Brahmins, low-caste artisans, Mohammedans, and Anglo-Indians seated in one congenial group on the blastfurnace sand-beds; Brahmins next to *kshatriyas* (the warrior caste) and *vaisyas* (artisan caste) next to *sudras* (the old slave caste)—all working side by side on the production line. I have seen a Mohammedan take a whiff of a pipe filled with tobacco or hemp and pass it to his neighbour, a high-caste Hindu. The Hindu would in turn pass it to a low-caste Hindu. I have seen Brahmins during a cholera epidemic tending the sick absolutely without discrimination.

It took Europe roughly a thousand years to free herself from the fetters of feudalism. The process will not have taken much more than fifty years in India—if industry continues to permeate the general life of the country. Fifty years ago, a Brahmin would not enter your dining-room when food was being served. Today he accepts your invitation to dine. But he brings his own cook, who prepares his vegetarian meal over a separate fire. He will eat with you, but he will not eat your food. It won't be long, I hope, before he will leave his cook at home and share at least the vegetable part of your meal.

Some of the Indians' own new awareness of the evils of the venerable Indian caste system, derived from ancient Vedic classifications of society, has been brought about by Mahatma Gandhi, who went, so far as to surround himself with Untouchables and to adopt one as his son. But there are many in India among the class which the Tatas may be taken to represent, who revere Gandhi for his sanctity and his sincerity, yet are themselves too dynamic in their thinking to have full faith in non-violence.

It is frequently said that the Congress Party, with or without Gandhi at its head, is supported by the moneyed commercial interests of India. I can only speak of the Tata attitude. The Tata family have always been empire-minded. They do, on the other hand, want to see India a self-governing dominion. So, feeling that eventually the Congress Party will win dominion status for India, the Tatas give the Congress a helping hand in a quiet way.

Like all big, forceful families, the Tatas had one member whose political activities were embarrassing. He was Shapurji Saklatwalla, the same man who tramped the hills with Sir Dorab Tata in Mayurbhanj State at Gurum in search of suitable ore veins. He was the son of Jamshedjee's sister. Later Shapurji was sent to London for Tata's, while his cousin, Sir Nowroji Saklatwalla, remained as chairman of Tata Sons. Shapurji had always been interested in labour. While he was in London, by a pronounced talent for fiery and persuasive oratory, Shapurji won parliamentary election in 1922 to represent North Battersea—as a Communist. He was, however, an able man, and was re-elected at least once on the same ticket.

It was disturbing to the Tatas to have an active and prominent Communist, in the family. Most of them were baronets, who had therefore sworn loyalty to their King-Emperor. Also they were sure that if England withdrew from India, the Japanese imperialists would take over as quickly as they could manage it and strip India to the bone.

Indians frequently refer to Jamshedpur as the Pittsburgh of the East. We always correct them. Jamshedpur is the Gary of the East. And the two great steel towns have a natural affinity for one another. Gary was built amid the barren sand dunes of Indiana. Jamshedpur sprang up right in the heart of an Indian jungle. Ground was broken for them both at about the same time. Both towns had a period when they were wide-open—there was a "Patch" in each place where the sky was the limit.

Three general managers of Tata's came from Gary, Temple W. Tutwiler, Barton Shover, and myself. Two assistant general superintendents were Gary men, W. S. McNabb and Thomas H. Clifford. They brought dozens of Gary mill-men with them. In 1914, when we were having our troubles with the German steel men, and the open-hearth furnace superintendent had to be replaced, Charles Page Perin got Tom Kenvin, superintendent or No. 3 open-hearth plant at Gary, to come out to India along with twenty or thirty other Americans. Tom had been with Carnegie Steel before he went to Gary. He was a quiet man, but when he said something, you knew he meant it. Kenvin was a wizard at his job, and he had the old open hearth going in no time. On second thought, it wasn't only that he was a wizard, he worked like a son-of-a-gun. You could never find him in his office. But you could see his tall, slender figure going through the gates to the mills between five and six o'clock in the morning. And many a night he'd finally knock off work at nine or ten to plod slowly home for a few hours' sleep. And he was no youngster.

The other Tom, Tom Clifford, was another man who lived on the job. In 1928 the duplex-steel plant wasn't pulling its weight. Frank Estep went to Gary and got Clifford. Soon after he got to Jamshedpur the duplex department commenced to produce tonnages unsurpassed at Lackawanna, Gary, South Chicago, or Bethlehem.

For donkey's years it was the custom for a crowd to gather in our bungalow for dinner on Sunday evening. Foreign mail arrived on Sunday morning as a rule, so everybody had news from home. A lot of the fellows there were former Gary men. We talked Gary most of the time, and I must say our wives were pretty patient about it. We talked of William Gleason, the stocky, ruddy-faced, grand old man who was in charge of that greatest of steel plants from the time ground was broken for it until he died twenty-five years later. Mr Gleason always called us proudly his "boys".

"Dammit, my boys are always leaving me to go to India," he'd fume. "Of course Tata's can pay 'em higher wages. They don't have the labour costs we do. Just as I get 'em trained, by God, off they go—and the best ones, too. It's that Tutwiler's fault, blast his soul!"

Once in a while a local story would supersede Gary as a topic of conversation, although not for long. There was the famous affair of the chamber-pot. On a Saturday night we had a gala at the Beldih Club. The temperature had dropped all the way down to 110 degrees. I mean it was hot. But the music was the best, the wines were old and mellow, and we were all having a very fine time. Two Tata men, Al Hirst, one of our superintendents, and Billy Marshall, the Cockney wag, were at top form. Marshall found an old-fashioned chamber-pot somewhere in one of the rooms, and taking it carefully out to the parking lot, opened Al Hirst's car and placed the pot in the driver's seat.

When Al decided to leave and arrived at the parking lot, a big Daimler was pulling into the space next to his car, filled with a party dressed to the teeth and ready for a big evening. Al saw the pot as he got in. He nonchalantly picked it up and sailed it through the car window into the Daimler, where it landed on the plump lap of a rather stiff-necked British lady of fashion. There was hell to pay.

The next night at our bungalow, we heard from Billy Marshall why the lady hadn't been able to pass the thing off in a spirit of fun. "It wasn't the pot itself that annoyed Lady—," he said. "She was mad because she thought somebody had dug up the story of her past. You see, she started life as a chambermaid in the Queen's Hotel in Birmingham!"

Then there was the time my wife left her most prized possession, a beautiful new hat of dusty pink felt, trimmed with aigrette feathers, lying on the bar at the Beldih Club while we went in to lunch. It was a holiday, and two convivial spirits who had begun celebrating early started an argument about just how long a bowlful of brandy would actually burn. The only container handy was my wife's hat. When the crown was brimming with brandy, they lighted it. Just then we returned from lunch. I gathered that my wife was less interested in the scientific aspect of the experiment that she was in the sodden, twisted mass of stinking felt and feathers which was all that remained of her lovely new bonnet.

A lot of our Sunday night talk was of death or the narrow escapes from death of the men we had worked with and liked. For steel men work, play, and die violently. When I left Gary to go out to India, the boys gave me a farewell party at Ted Binson's place.

The bar there was 120 feet long. Ted always had twelve bar men on duty, one for every ten feet of bar. Each man kept a big Colt below the bar top within easy reach, especially on pay days.

Among the best lads in the farewell party was Nemo, who later disappeared somewhere in Alaska. Jim died a few years later under a pile of red-hot coke. Harry, who had played on Gordon Brown's squad at Yale, found a grave in the Pacific, over the ship's side.

Walter was at Ted's with a friend. Not long after, Gary's old Number 5 blew up. When it came down it landed on Walter. His friend went to the top of a blast furnace to work on a bell rod. The furnace gas overcame him. He fell to his death on the large bell. Billy Blundell was at Ted's. He had a close call. That was in Jamshedpur, after Billy had followed me to India.

In 1926 Billy was working on a break-out on C furnace. To get at the break-out he decided to blast away the concrete which surrounded the furnace. He drilled a few holes and fired them. Then he started tamping dynamite into another hole, and it blew up. At the hospital they found he had about one chance in ten thousand. A piece of concrete larger than a pigeon's egg had lodged in one lung. There were lumps of concrete stuck all through his chest and legs, and his face was gashed with particles.

Our chief medical officer, Dr. Chakravarty, decided that Billy would die on the table if he tried to remove the concrete from the lungs. If the lump was cement it would dissolve, if it was stone it could wait to be removed when Billy was stronger. Chakravarty put Billy under an inhaler and treated him for pneumonia. Sir Frank Connor, then India's foremost surgeon, rushed to Jamshedpur. After his examination he said, "I agree with the treatment entirely. A lung operation in the near future would undoubtedly be fatal. I am proud of your chief medical officer. He was one of my honour students in the medical school."

Chakravarty is only one of the many fine Indian physicians I have known. The cement did dissolve, and Bill is still in India. He must like the place, because he hasn't been home on leave since 1922!

Of course, we old Gary men are apt to spin so many yarns about the plant and about each other we give the impression that we were solely responsible for the success of Tata's. That isn't true. Jack Peterson, who took charge of the company from Bombay in 1925, was a Britisher.

A high official in the Government once called Peterson the rudest Englishman who had ever come to India. Others claimed that Peterson had heard of the remark and ever after tried to live up to it. Personally I always found him the kindest-hearted Scot I've ever known. And he didn't mind taking a chance on a man he trusted. He once gave me a power of attorney, authorizing me to sign contracts up to two million pounds sterling.

Another Britisher, F. C. Temple, an engineer, laid out the expanded town of Jamshedpur in 1919 so well that almost no changes have been necessary as the town became a city. Temple was a son of an Archbishop of Canterbury and a brother of the late Archbishop of Canterbury. He seemed the best possible person to act as starter at our races. He made a good one.

The all-round abilities of Harry Chew, also from England, made him invaluable to the company. Chew had had charge of the rolling programme of a big British steel company. He took over Tata's original merchant mill, planning the rolling of sections to lose the least possible time between roll changes. For mills make no profits when they're idle. Successively, Chew was superintendent of ore mines and quarries, acting sales manager, and finally assistant general manager until his untimely death two years ago.

So, proud as I am of the American share in the success of Tata's, the British were just as responsible for it in their own ways. And not only the ones who came out for a few years. Some of the best lie buried in the quiet little graveyard we call Jackal Square. They and the Americans who lie with them are the fallen part of the army of workers who, side by side with their Indian colleagues and Indian pupils, helped to build and extend the Tata enterprises. In peace-time the company employs 70,000 people. It contributes $5,000,000 to the Government in taxes and railway charges. It obeys the behest of Jamshedjee Tata to preserve, undimmed, the ideal of public service.

As in the past three years Dunkirk and Lidice have become more than mere place names, as they symbolize bravery and martyrdom to millions of people, so in a smaller, a humbler way, Gary is more to her old "boys" than a steel plant. Gary is to us a hard taskmaster, and at the same time a foster mother.

There was a unique camaraderie among Gary men when Teddy Roosevelt was forming the Bull Moose Party, when Tom Notts was Mayor of Gary and the town was wide-open, when every building on Broadway from the railroad tracks at 9th Avenue to 14th Avenue and all the way across to Jefferson Street was a bar—and every bar-room had a card table or a roulette wheel.

Some day in my lifetime, perhaps when I get back from China, I want to get all the old Gary Indians together in Gary, Indiana, for an old home week. And we will feel at home, too, for Gary always welcomes her sons back again.

I wonder what ever happened to the Patch? I wonder if the Red Onion still stands, the three bright-red, two-storey shacks which housed the overflow workers some thirty years ago, down on the hot yellow sand?

I wonder if the tumble brushes still drift and blow among the windy dunes?

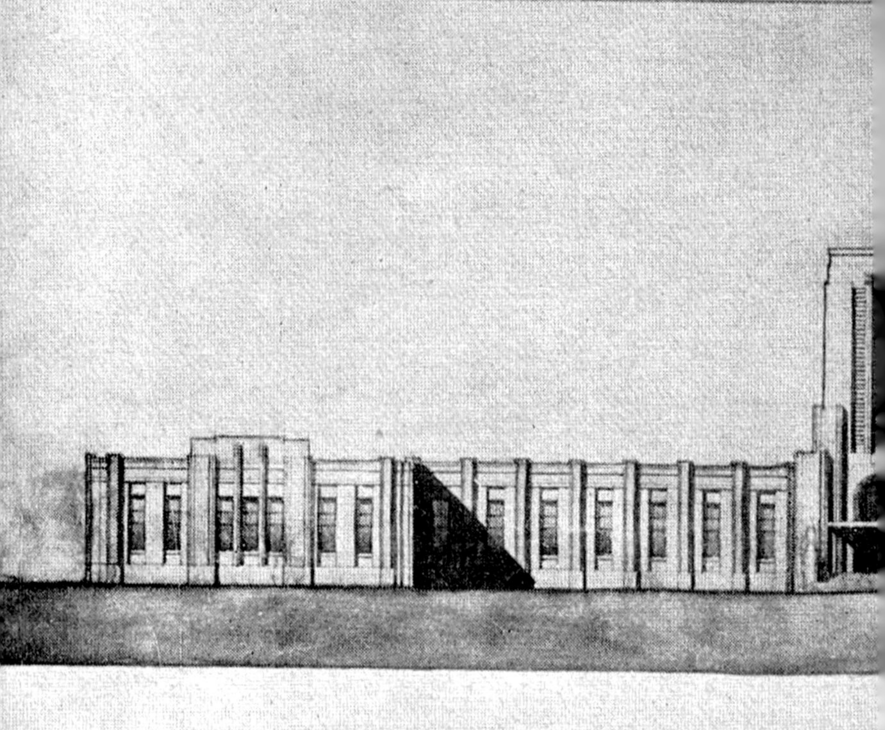

PROPOSED NEW CONTROL AND RESE
INCORPORATING METALLURGICAL TEST HOUSE INSPECTION C
FOR
THE TATA IRON AND STEEL COMPANY
JAMSHEDPUR B.N.RY.